water and corn[illegible] boil.
Stir in 1 tsp soda [illegible] 3
boiling milk, salt [illegible]
tb butter. Bring to a boil and serve.
Serves 12 people.

Hamburg Steaks

Run 1 lb. lean beef through chopper twice.
Season with salt, pepper + finely chopped
onion + ½ tsp nutmeg. Mix in one slightly
beaten egg. Shape into flat cakes and
fry in deep fat.

Canned Chicken

Kill clean + put in tub of water over
night with a little salt to draw out
blood. Drain well, cut up + skin. Joint
legs at main joint and again at
center. Cut all meat off breast. Pack in
jars. Put carcasses on in steep pan,
cover with water + boil till scraps of
meat are cooked. Have jars sterilized.
Put on top of each a small tsp salt and
a little minced onion. Fill the bottles with
strained liquor from bones, put on rubbers
and lids, leaving a turn or two loose. Put
in boiler and boil for 3 hours. As soon as
cool enough screw tops tight. (Skim fat off
water as clean as you can) and season
with salt + pepper.

Chicken Mould

Clean scraps off carcasses + run through through
chopper. To every 7 cups ground meat use 3½ tsp
salt, some pepper and onion. Dissolve a box

Aunt Maud's Recipe Book

water and tomatoes + bring to boil. Stir in 1 tsp soda + strain. Add, stirring, salt + pepper, 2 level tbl butter. Bring to a boil and serve. Serves 12 people.

Hamburg Steaks

Run 1 lb. lean beef through chopper twice. Season with salt, pepper + finely chopped onion + 1/2 tsp nutmeg. Mix in one slightly beaten egg. Shape into flat cakes and fry in deep fat.

Canned Chicken

Kill, clean + put in tub of water over night with a little salt to draw out blood. Drain well, cut up + skin. Joint legs at main joint and again at ankle. Cut all meat off breast. Pack in jars. Put carcasses on in stew pan, cover with water + boil till scraps of meat are cooked. Have jars sterilized. Put on top of each a small tsp salt and a little minced onion. Fill the bottles with strained liquor from bones, put on rubbers and lids, leaving a turn or two loose. Put in boiler and boil for 3 hours. As soon as cool enough screw tops tight. (Skim fat off water as clean as you can) and season with salt + pepper.

Chicken Mould

Clean scraps off carcases + run them through chopper. To every 2 cups ground meat use 3 1/2 tsp

Pork Mock Duck & Apples.

Select two large pork tenderloins, have them split open & flattened. Prepare a dressing, place it between the tenderloins and sew them together. Arrange strips of [illegible] ... in the butter till they are very rich and brown. [illegible]. Serve as a garnish about the duck. Make gravy from fat in pan. [illegible] apples [illegible] be at a pinch.

If I had not been a poor devil of an author
I think I would have made an excellent cook.

L.M. Montgomery

Lima Bean Supper Dish.

Soak lima beans overnight & boil till somewhat tender. Place in baking dish. Season with salt & pepper. A little tomato sauce may be added if liked. Lay on top some strips of fat bacon. Bake in moderate oven half an hour or until beans are tender.

Aunt Maud's Recipe Book

from the kitchen of

L. M. Montgomery

Elaine Crawford & Kelly Crawford

Moulin

Moulin Publishing Limited
P. O. Box #560
Norval, Ontario
Canada L0P 1K0

First Edition

For Canadian Cataloguing in Publication Data
please contact the National Library of Canada

ISBN 1-896867-01-4

Jacket and book design by Counterpunch/Linda Gustafson
Printed and bound in Canada

Contents

Preface

When I visited Dr. Stuart Macdonald in the years before his death in 1982, he often spoke of a pie that his mother used to make. It was called a mock-cherry pie. "What's *in* it?" I asked him, thinking of the "mock turkey" that my husband made, substituting all kinds of other meats for the turkey. What could one substitute for cherries that tasted like cherries?

He told me how his mother would make small mock cherry pies and bring tins of them to him at the University of Toronto, where he was studying medicine. One of his best friends there was Lem Prowse, another medical student, from P.E.I. The two of them awaited these tins with enormous anticipation. It didn't take long for them to eat them all, and then they would persuade his mother to make a fresh supply. Stuart had never forgotten those mock-cherry pies, despite the fact that the recipe had been lost when his mother died in 1942.

I puzzled over the frequency with which these pies came into his memory. It pointed to the role that food plays in a family – a mother provides food to give sustenance. She also provides it to show love. The recipe had come from Prince Edward Island, just as she had, and connected her past, her son, his friend, and her in a web of caring and pleasure – pleasure in Island delicacies, pleasure in sharing them with others.

L.M.Montgomery (Mrs. Ewan Macdonald in private life) was a very busy woman, but she was not too busy to make treats for her son and bring them to him. She understood very well how much human pleasure comes from good food. And she was right – till the end of his life, he remembered those mock-cherry pies, and associated them with his mother.

A few days before he died suddenly in September 1982, Dr. Macdonald had been to our house for an evening of bridge with my husband, our family doctor, and a friend. From time to time, these four card sharks got together; they played cards and tried to outquote each other, particularly with Shakespeare. Dr. Macdonald knew his Shakespeare well, as did my husband who taught Renaissance Literature at the University of Guelph. Dr. John Woodger and Father Gus Arthurs had sharp minds for witticisms and special quotations too.

Unfortunately, Dr. Macdonald had been feeling increasingly poorly for several weeks, or perhaps months, but he had not wanted to cancel this card game. I was worried about him because I could see he was unwell, but I did not know how serious it was, nor did he, even though he was a medical doctor. My only thought was to take him back home as quickly as possible the next morning. But he wanted to go through Norval so he could once again see where he had lived from age ten until he was grown.

When we entered the little hamlet of Norval, he asked me to slow down. He looked at the houses and talked fondly of who had lived in them. He spoke of the Credit River and his old swimming hole. I could see him disappearing before my eyes: he was retreating into the past and reliving his boyhood. He told me how happy he had been there, what a wonderful town it had been in his boyhood. He talked of how he always slept out in his tent down by the river bank through the hot summers. His mother would sometimes slip down at dusk to visit with him. They would sit there together talking, listening to the crickets, the flowing river, and the other night sounds. And she would bring him sweets to eat. "Mock-cherry pie?" I ventured.

He asked me to stop the car, and he walked by himself down to the river, and lingered along its banks. Dr. Macdonald understood that his mother had found comfort in those private visits with him down by the soothing river. I have never seen someone so abstracted in memory, and so happy at being alone: he was a man taking leave of a scene he had loved, of memories precious to him. He walked further down to his old swimming hole. When he returned, he did not talk for a long time, and we drove on in silence. He was exhausted, and in pain. A few days later, he died.

There was a sad irony in our last mention of the mock-cherry pie. After a lifetime of remembering that pie, and wishing that he had the recipe so that Ruth, his wife, could make it for him and their family, we knew that the lost recipe was just about to turn up.

Here is the story: Stuart and Ruth had invited Anita Webb to their house some time earlier so that I could talk to her about when she lived with his mother. (Dr. Macdonald has asked me to do the official biography of his mother, as well as edit the journals, and he was helping introduce me to people who had known his mother.) Anita had come up from Cavendish as a young girl to visit with the Reverend and Mrs. Macdonald, and she stayed to help Maud for a spell.

Some other children of Myrtle and Ernest Webb also came up: Marion, who married Murray Laird, a son of one of Norval's prominent families; Keith, who went into the greenhouse business in Norval. These young people had all been raised in what is now the "Anne of Green Gables" house in Cavendish, but like so many Islanders of the time, they moved to central Canada to find opportunity. And like so many others, they settled where they knew someone. In this case, it was their cousin, Mrs. L.M. Montgomery Macdonald, the famous authoress who lived in Norval.

Like all of her clan on Prince Edward Island, Anita Webb was already a splendid cook, even though she was only a young woman. After working for Maud, she went on to a career in professional cooking in Toronto. During her final years, Maud Montgomery decided to recopy the cookbook which held all of the old family recipes – from the Webbs, the Macneills, the Campbells, the Montgomerys – as well as those from Island friends, and from Leaskdale and Norval parishioners. As she recopied her cookbook, she crossed out the original recipes. Then she gave the discarded cookbook to Anita who used it in her professional life.

Many of those recipes have been eaten by the scores of Toronto young people Anita cooked for variously at Upper Canada College, Knox College, and Willard Hall. As for the new cookbook – the one into which the recipes were copied – it has disappeared. Perhaps it was sold at auction when the 210 Riverside Drive house (in Toronto) was emptied in 1942, after Montgomery's death. Perhaps it was discarded.

After I talked to Anita that summer evening at the Macdonalds' house, I drove her home. On the way, I asked her if she had ever heard of this recipe that Dr. Macdonald talked about. That's when I discovered that she had Maud's old cookbook. "Does it have the recipe for something called 'mock-cherry pie'?" I asked, hoping against hope that it did. "Yes," she had told me, and she promised to lend me the cookbook. I told this to Dr. Macdonald, who was delighted. He looked forward to eating that pie again as soon as the long-lost recipe reappeared. But his death intervened.

In time, Anita Webb passed the cookbook along to her niece, Elaine Laird Crawford, through Marion Webb Laird, who was Anita's sister and Elaine's mother. That seemed an especially satisfying destination, given two facts: (1) that Maud had promoted the romance and marriage that produced Elaine and (2) that Elaine, with her husband Bob Crawford, ran a noted bakery, restaurant, and food establishment in Norval. I was delighted when the Crawfords undertook the work of testing and updating (as necessary) the recipes for publication in this book.

Many of those Webb and Montgomery family recipes in Maud's original cookbook had for years been served at "Crawford's." I had eaten there a few times, and I noticed that people came from miles around to buy baked goods. Torontians would drive out on the weekends that the Crawfords made their famous "butterscotch pie," for instance. I doubted that people knew that they were eating some of the Island recipes which had come up with the Webbs and L.M.Montgomery. They were probably also eating a few recipes that Montgomery's beloved cousin Frederica Campbell, a professional Home Economist, collected during the summer she studied at the University of Guelph, where Maud's original journals and much of her other memorablia now reside in the Archives. However collected, Montgomery's recipes represent what she loved: good food and good company to eat it with.

And that's the end of the tale of how this book came to be, and how it brings together Prince Edward Island and Ontario, and all of the people who have eaten Anita Webb's or the Crawfords' good cooking. Or those who have memories of the delicious cakes Maud Montgomery served up at church socials. Some of the Norval and Leaskdale parishioners may find their family recipes in this book. Our pleasure in food links us all! And, as L.M. Montgomery and her son both would say, "Well, there you *are*!"

Mary Henley Rubio
Professor of English
University of Guelph
Guelph, Ontario, N1G 2W1

Co-Editor, with Elizabeth Waterston, of *The Selected Journals of L. M. Montgomery, Volumes 1, 2, and 3* (Oxford University Press, 1985, 1987, 1992), and of *Writing a Life: L. M. Montgomery* (ECW Press, 1995); Editor of *Harvesting Thistles: The Textual Garden of L. M. Montgomery, Essays on Her Novels and Journals* (CCP, 1994).

July 1996

Scrambled Eggs.

1 large can evaporated milk 2 tbs butter, 6 eggs beaten, ½ tsp salt-pepper. Put all ingredients in double boiler & cook while stirring until thickened. Serve with parsley garnish. Nice served with green peas

---

Dried Beef.

For every 20 lbs. beef use 1 pt salt, 1 tsp salt petre ¼ lb. brown sugar, mix & then divide in 3 equal parts. Rub one part into the beef on 3 successive days. Let it lie for a week in the brine it will make, turning every day. Then hang it up in a dry place till it stops dripping. Hang then in a cool dry place after rubbing it over with red pepper

---

Spiced Beef.

For 20 lbs beef (round or flank) take ¼ lb. brown sugar, 1 pt salt, 1 tsp salt-petre ¼ lb. allspice ¼ lb. white pepper, 1 oz mace, 1 oz cloves ⅛ oz cayenne pepper 1 oz cinnamon. Mix and divide into 4 equal portions. Rub one into meat every day for 4 days. Then turn every day for four days in pickle which will have formed. Take it out. If flank, roll tightly and cord it well & hang it up to dry for a week or so. If hung sew in a cloth & hang. Boil 4 hours.

Introduction

"I HAVE NEVER been one of those who consider a 'liking for a tasty bite' something to be rather ashamed of. Frankly, I'm very fond of a good table. I keep one myself and I like to sit down to one. It is an old Montgomery tradition and when I hear anyone say 'I don't care what I have to eat,' I conclude that individual is either lying, or is a pale anaemic creature of very little use and no charm or force in the world. And I have mostly found that this conclusion was borne out by the facts of the case." – *L.M. Montgomery*

Green Gables, home of Ernest and Myrtle Webb and family.

Lucy Maud Montgomery is famous throughout the world for her engaging characters and captivating tales: her extraordinary writing abilities have produced such well loved stories as *Anne of Green Gables* and the *Emily* series. Less well known is her considerable talent in the kitchen; she was an excellent cook and took great interest in good food. In Montgomery's day considerably more time was taken up with growing, harvesting, preserving and preparing food than at present, and with a busy writing career, two children and the reponsibilities of a minister's wife, Maud required the help of a maid to keep the house in order. But she loved to cook, especially when entertaining, and relished the freedom of her own kitchen when her maid had a day off. Her handwritten recipe book, treasured as it has been passed down in our family, provides a rare glimpse of food and its preparation in the early 1900s. More importantly, her recipe book allows us to step into Lucy Maud Montgomery's kitchen, to smell the cakes she baked and taste the stews she served to family and friends.

Aunt Maud in the kitchen of the Leaskdale Manse, in a self-portrait taken by double exposure. The calendar date is May, 1922.

The heritage of food is an important cultural tradition, made powerful by our never-ending need for sustenance. Montgomery's recipe book reflects a sharing of recipes between family and community; you'll find recipes from Mrs. Barraclough, Marion Webb, Frede Campbell, Mrs. MacPherson, Myrtle (Macneill) Webb and others in this collection. Prepared foods were unavailable in the early 1900s and people expected, as a matter of course, to prepare all their food, from bread and preserves to stews and wines. A substantial selection of easily workable recipes was a necessity, not merely a point of pride. Families kept recipes alive with their constant use through successive generations, no doubt altering them as the supply of ingredients changed. Montgomery's highly developed sense of propriety and the dedication she brought to her duties as a minister's wife meant that she was unfailingly prepared for Session meetings, Sunday School picnics, and visits to or from members of the congregation with the appropriate salads, cakes, jellies, biscuits or cookies.

L.M. Montgomery's recipe book came to my mother, Elaine Crawford, through her mother, Marion (Webb) Laird, and her aunt, Anita Webb, the two eldest daughters of Montgomery's third cousin, Myrtle Macneill. Myrtle lived at Green Gables, the real life house that became *Anne's* imaginary home in *Anne of Green Gables*, through her teen years with her great aunt and uncle, Margaret and David Macneill. Many locals have assumed that the characters of Matthew and Marilla in *Anne of Green Gables* were inspired by David and Margaret Macneill, who were similar in personality as well as circumstance, although Montgomery flatly denied this. Myrtle married Ernest C. Webb, and after several years, at Margaret and David's request, the young couple returned to live at Green Gables, taking over the farm chores and caring for the elderly brother and sister through their declining years.

Aunt Maud and Lorraine Webb

Ernest and Myrtle lived for 39 years at Green Gables, raising a family of five children: Marion, Keith, Anita, Lorraine, and Pauline. Green Gables was never a happier place than during the years that the Webb children were growing up. Fun was as-they-made-it, but found everywhere, even while the chores of farming and preparing meals claimed a good part of each day. The shore was close by, spruce gum was found easily in the neighbouring woods, and there were countless ferny nooks and hollows to explore along the wood lanes. Lover's Lane, the exquisitely beautiful and soul-satisfying retreat of Montgomery's youth, ran from Webb's laneway to a back field. It was a delight-filled playground for the Webb children too, with its gurgling brook and secret corners. Nearly every summer Maud returned to the Island for a holiday, making the rounds of friends and family, staying a few days with each. The Webbs always enjoyed her visits to Green Gables to reacquaint herself with Lover's Lane and other favourite haunts.

With the publication of *Anne of Green Gables* in 1908, Montgomery's readers began to take an interest in Green Gables, travelling to see the spot where an imaginary Anne Shirley had so many adventures. No one minded that the lively Webb family actually lived there. In a testament to Montgomery's captivating writing abilities, readers have always felt the need to stand at the doors of Green Gables and be a little closer to entering the enchanted world of her characters. Plain old Island hospitality invited the strangers in to see the house, then to have tea, and finally to stay. Before long, the Webbs were taking in "boarders" – people who had come to the Island for a holiday, whose curiosity had led them to Green Gables and who made acquaintance with the Webbs. Folks would stay for a week or two, and often return year after year.

The far end of Lover's Lane, one of Aunt Maud's favourite haunts on the Green Gables farm.

During this time, Montgomery had married the Reverend Ewan Macdonald, and had moved with him in 1911 to a charge in Leaskdale, Ontario, where their sons, Chester and Stuart, were born. After fourteen years, Macdonald accepted a call to the Norval and Union charge, and in 1926, they moved into the Presbyterian manse in the picturesque village of Norval. Maud quickly grew to love Norval, with its stand of pines on Russell's hill and the Credit River winding its way through the village. The manse was handsome, and was the first home she had with electricity. In 1927 Maud went home to the Island for a visit, and when she returned to Norval she brought along Marion Webb for a holiday. Maud was quite fond of Marion; she sensed in the younger woman a shared sensitivity for the natural beauty of their island home, and liked her happy, optimistic nature. It was during this vacation that Marion met Murray Laird, the most eligible bachelor in Norval. He was quite taken with her, and they spent every possible minute together. Murray Laird's family owned a farm on Norval's east hill, having settled the area several generations back. Murray's father Alfred and his brothers were carpenters and builders as well as farmers; they had built the Presbyterian Church in Norval in 1878, and the Lairds were members of the congregation. Maud thought Murray would be an appropriate match for Marion but did not press the issue when Marion's holiday ended and she returned to the Island.

Ernest and Myrtle lavished as much time and care on their flower gardens as they did on their vegetable garden.

But Marion and Murray had fallen in love. In spite of the distance that separated them, their romance deepened and in 1934 they were happily married at the manse in a ceremony performed by Ewan Macdonald. From that time on, Marion, being one of the "tribe of Joseph," was a constant companion to Maud, who forever missed Prince Edward Island and her kin.

Marion and Murray had four children: Patricia, Ian, Elaine, and Peter. Elaine married Robert Crawford, and together we operate *Crawford's*, a quality renowned village bakery and distinctive food shop, where clientele have gathered fine foods for the past 25 years. Located on the southern half of the original Laird farm, *Crawford's* has kept the tradition of excellence in cooking, baking, and preserve making that had its beginning in old family recipes. L.M. Montgomery's original recipe book has been a source of inspiration, particularly as a reminder of the care and respect that good food requires.

One of Maud's recipes for Fruit Cake has found favour with customers at *Crawford's*; because of its unusual ingredients we're guessing that it is a very old recipe that may have been modified even before it came to Maud. This cake was served once again at an afternoon tea at the manse during Norval's Montgomery Christmas Weekend, a celebration of her birthday (Nov. 30) which the village has held annually since 1993.

The Crawford family invite you to share part of our rich food heritage with *Aunt Maud's Recipe Book.* We have tested the recipes that appear in this book, sometimes determining quantities of ingredients or baking times where Maud hasn't given specific direction, sometimes offering our suggestions for beneficial alterations. The recipes appear exactly as they are in her handwritten ledger; our suggestions and clarifications appear in italic. In each chapter we have arranged recipes to form a menu that you could serve, and have provided alternatives that could be substituted. Our selection of recipes is unique to an era in Canadian cooking; you'll find their simplicity reflects ingredient availability, the necessity for innovation (e.g., Mock Cherry Pie), and the lack of many outside cultural influences in the early 1900s. Slip into Montgomery's kitchen, and bake some of her cakes, taste her biscuits and jam, and serve her roasts and stews. She would be pleased to know that you share her "liking for a tasty bite"!

Looking down the Credit River in Norval.

Afternoon Tea at the Manse

Norval manse was frequently the setting for afternoon teas. Because of Ewan's professional relationships and obligations, Maud's involvement with the Women's Institute, and her large circle of personal friends, she often entertained in the afternoon. Referring to one such occasion, she wrote, "I have always enjoyed such affairs. I like to make out a nice menu and get out my pretty linens and dishes and give everyone a pleasant time."

Marion and Murray Laird, 1934.

Regular visits to congregation members would usually be at their homes, but it was common practice in the 1930s for couples to come to the manse to be wed. Generally the bride and groom attended alone, or with a minimal number of parents or friends, and Ewan performed the ceremony in the parlour. Although a marriage at the manse was often a perfunctory affair, Maud would make more of the occasion for people she knew well and liked: "All day I worked hard getting ready a supper for Ada Marquis and her husband, who came here at five this evening to be married. Ordinarily of course I don't get tea for the couples who come here to be married. But Ada has always been a particular friend of mine.... So I made salad and cake and biscuits etc. and fixed up a pretty table with pink-shaded candles."

Maud took great delight in the budding romance between Marion Webb and Murray Laird during Marion's first visit to Norval, and quickly reneged on an earlier vow to stay out of match-making. In 1930 she invited Marion to Norval for the winter, hoping to further the relationship that appeared to have stalled with the difficulties of distance between Prince Edward Island and Ontario. She watched with satisfaction as their romance blossomed, was pleased with Murray's devotion, and was as happy and full of plans for Marion as if she had been her own daughter. When the couple were to be married, Maud threw herself into a flurry of preparations, even though only she and Mrs. Laird were in attendance due to the recent death of Murray's father. The day before the wedding, she made a cake, salad, jelly, mock chicken and layer cookies. She went next door to the MacPherson's, four spinster sisters who excelled and took great pride with their gardens, for flowers to decorate the parlour. At the appointed hour the following afternoon, Murray and Mrs. Laird arrived for the ceremony, and Maud's delectable tea followed.

The Reverend Ewan Macdonald and Maud on a boat excursion on Georgian Bay, 1930.

Afternoon Tea at the Manse

MENU

Chicken Sandwiches

Mrs. Fraser's Sandwiches

Orange Biscuits with Plum Jam

Tea Punch

Ginger Cordial

Marion's Orange Cake

Mrs. MacPherson's Gingersnaps

Layer Cookies

Brown Sugar Ice Cream

Chicken Sandwiches

1 c	chicken, *cooked and* minced
1 c	celery, finely chopped
2	eggs, hard boiled and chopped
12	olives, chopped
	salad dressing to moisten

Mix all together and moisten with dressing. Spread between buttered slices *of bread with their crusts removed.* Veal or pork may replace chicken. *Makes 9 full sandwiches that may each be cut into four triangles.*

Mrs. Fraser's Sandwiches

Although not described as a ribbon sandwich, we suspect these sandwiches were constructed as such. An unsliced loaf of bread was trimmed of crusts and cut horizontally into long slices. After stacking slices with filling and setting overnight, the assembled loaf would be sliced vertically and attractively arranged on a pretty plate. The amounts given will fill one loaf of bread, serving 12.

$\frac{1}{2}$ lb	butter
$\frac{1}{2}$ lb	cheese *(cream cheese)*
1 c	pimentoes

Soften butter and cheese and mix well. Then add chopped pimento. Spread on bread quite generously. Put slices on top of each other and press well. Tie in waxed paper and wrap in damp towel all night. Cut in slices. Nice with alternate brown and white slices.

Plum and orange are two flavours that complement each other nicely. While each of these recipes is great on its own, we recommend trying them together!

Orange Biscuits

2 c	flour
4 tsp	baking powder
½ tsp	salt
¾ c	milk
4 tbsp	shortening
½ tbsp	grated orange rind
	juice of one orange

Mix and sift flour, B.P. *(baking powder)* and salt. Cut in shortening with a fork. Add orange rind and *enough* milk to make a soft dough. Roll out on a slightly floured board to ½ inch thickness. Cut with a biscuit cutter. *Arrange on cookie sheet.*

Dip half size pieces of loaf sugar *(cubes)* in orange juice. Put a piece of sugar on each biscuit and press in. Bake in hot oven (425°F) 10 to 15 minutes.

Plum Jam

Weigh fruit *(plums)* and take ⅓ as much apples. Peel apples and cut up in small pieces.

Take pound for pound of sugar and enough water to dissolve. When boiling put in apples and boil till soft. Then put in plums and let come to a boil.

May we suggest:

3 lb	*fresh pitted prune plums*
1 lb	*apples*
4 lb	*sugar*
	water

Bring sugar and water to the boil. Add chopped apples and cook until soft.
Add plums and boil for 20 to 25 minutes, stirring frequently.
Pour into sterilized jars and seal.

On a hot summer day guests may well appreciate a tall cold glass of this tea punch more than a hot cup of tea.

Tea Punch

2 oz	black tea
	(2 oz loose tea = 1/2 c loose tea = 12 two-cup tea bags)
8 c	boiling water
1 3/4 c	sugar
	juice of 1 orange
	juice of 2 lemons
1 c	currant juice
1 c	raspberry juice

Pour boiling water over 2 oz of the best black tea and let stand 5 minutes. Strain off and add 2 scant cups of sugar, the juice of one orange and 2 lemons, 1 cup currant juice and 1 cup raspberry juice. Chill and serve ice cold in tall glasses. Garnish each glass with a sprig of frosted mint. To make this dip *fresh* mint *leaves* in beaten egg white, then in powdered sugar and *set aside to* allow to harden.

On Tea Making

A china or crockery teapot is essential in making a good pot of tea. Warm the pot with hot water. Fill the kettle with cold water and bring to a rolling boil. Meanwhile, into the teapot put one tsp of loose tea leaves for each cup of tea plus one for the pot. As soon as the water boils, pour it over the tea. Let steep for 3 minutes, or, if personal preference dictates, up to 5 minutes. Strain through a silver or stainless steel strainer into individual cups, or decant through a stainer into a second warmed pot.

Tea that is served from a silver teapot should be first brewed in a crockery or china pot. Never use an aluminum tea pot or strainer; this metal will adversely affect the flavour.

If you wish to use tea bags, one bag per cup is the general rule, and they are easily removed after steeping. One-cup tea bags and two-cup tea bags are both available.

There are three main categories of tea: black, green and oolong. Black tea is the choice for afternoon tea, and Orange Pekoe is perhaps the best known blend within this category.

Milk, sugar, and thin lemon slices should accompany the tea table.

A refreshing drink on a hot summer's day!

Maud has two similar recipes for Ginger Cordial: one as given below and another using powdered ginger. Fresh ginger root came from Jamaica in Maud's day and was a frequently used flavouring for beverages, candies and cookies.

Ginger Cordial

6 lb	sugar
4 qt	water
2 oz	white ginger *root*, crushed and tied in muslin
8 tsp	powdered tartaric acid

Bring to a boil and boil until syrup becomes a little thick. Add 8 level tsp powdered tartaric acid. Makes 4 quarts. *Serve over ice, one part syrup with three parts water.*

We decided that this recipe would make a whole summer's supply, so our scaled down version is as follows.

3 3/4 c	*sugar*
4 c	*water*
1/2 oz	*crushed ginger root, in a muslin bag*
2 tsp	*cream of tartar*

Bring to a boil and simmer 10 minutes. Let cool slightly. Add 1 tsp cream of tartar. Keep in a jar in the refrigerator. Makes 5 cups.

Serve one part syrup to two parts soda over ice, with a twist of lime.

This recipe comes from Marion Webb, and was written on a very well-worn page in Maud's ledger. In spots her writing is illegible, requiring some guess-work and several trial runs. Marion herself tasted our final version, and says we've got it just right!

Marion's Orange Cake

½ c	butter
1 c	brown sugar
2	eggs
1 tsp	soda
½ c	sour milk
2 c	all purpose flour
1 tsp	salt
1 c	raisins
½ c	chopped walnuts (optional)
	one orange (rind and pulp)

Cream butter and sugar. Mix in well-beaten eggs.

Dissolve soda in the sour milk and add to mixture. *(½ c fresh milk may be soured by adding 1 tsp vinegar.)*

Add flour and salt. Chop the *entire* orange, remove seeds and run orange and raisins through chopper. *Or process in a food processor until finely chopped but not pureed.*

Add to mixture. Mix well. *Pour into large greased* loaf pan.

Bake at 350°F for 50 to 60 minutes.

The MacPherson sisters lived next door to the Presbyterian Church in Norval. The four sisters remained unmarried all of their lives, so we conclude this recipe is from their mother. It was Charlotte who accompanied Maud into Toronto every December to Woolworth's, where they purchased the necessary 100 or so presents for the Sunday School Christmas tree. They travelled on the radial train, boarding at its station atop the south hill of the village, known locally as Cemetery Hill. The radial was an electric railway that ran from Toronto to Guelph between 1917 and 1931; its elegant, dark green passenger cars with green plush seats carried Maud in both directions as she went about her business.

Mrs. MacPherson's Gingersnaps

Here is the original recipe as written in the recipe book; below, we recommend a smaller batch size with some adjustments.

1 c brown sugar
1 c lard or dripping
1 c syrup

Let these ingredients come to a boil together in a saucepan. When cool add 1 tbsp ginger, 1 tsp soda and enough flour to roll. Roll thin, cut in rounds, and bake in a hot oven. Cinnamon and cloves can be added if liked.

½ c brown sugar
½ c shortening
½ c molasses

Combine the above ingredients in a saucepan and bring to a boil. Cool to lukewarm. Add to the following ingredients that have been pre-mixed in a mixing bowl.

1 tbsp	*ginger*
1/2 tsp	*soda*
1/2 tsp	*salt*
1 tsp	*cinnamon*
1/2 tsp	*cloves*
2 c	*all purpose flour*

Mix well, turn out onto a floured board and roll 1/8 of an inch thick. Cut in rounds. Place on a greased cookie sheet and bake in a 325°F oven for 12 to 15 minutes.

Makes about 4 dozen 2-inch cookies. Store in a tin to retain crispness.

Maud must have liked these cookies; in her journal she often notes that she has made Layer Cookies for social events, including Marion Webb's wedding!

Layer Cookies

First Layer

½ c	crisco *(or other shortening)*
1 c	white sugar
2	eggs, beaten
½ tsp	vanilla
1 ½ c	pastry flour spooned into cup
1 tsp	baking powder
½ tsp	salt

Cream crisco and sugar. Add eggs and vanilla. Then flour sifted with salt and baking powder. Spread ½ inch thick over shallow *greased 9x13 inch* pan.

Second Layer

1	egg white
1 c	light brown sugar
½ tsp	vanilla
¾ c	chopped walnuts

Beat egg white till fluffy, fold in sugar, add vanilla. Spread over first layer. Sprinkle with walnuts. Bake 30 minutes in a moderate oven *350°F. Mark surface into squares while warm.* Cut in squares when cool.

In the method of this recipe Maud refers to the use of a hand-cranked ice cream freezer. Ice was shaved from blocks of ice which were stored under sawdust in the ice house and the shavings or "snow" were packed in the outer compartment of the ice cream freezer around the central container full of ingredients. Salt was added to the snow to accelerate freezing. Ice needed to be replaced part way through the freezing process. The crank had to be turned by hand constantly, until it could be turned no more. The ice cream was "ripened" by standing for several minutes before serving.

Brown Sugar Ice Cream

2 ½ c	milk
2 tbsp	flour
¼ c	*cold* water
2	eggs
¾ c	brown sugar
2 tsp	vanilla
1 c	cream

Scald the milk in the top part of a double boiler. Take out 1 cupful of hot milk and put it in a saucepan. Bring to a boil and stir into it the flour *which has been* mixed with the cold water until it runs freely. *Let cook briefly, stirring constantly. Stir into hot milk in top part of double boiler.*

Beat the eggs well with the brown sugar and beat this quickly into the hot milk in double boiler. Stir custard frequently for 15 minutes *as it cooks over simmering water. Cool.*

When cold strain *through a fine sieve* and add vanilla and cream.

This serves 8 people amply and would do for 10. Use 2 packings of snow but salt only once. No salt in packing with snow to ripen.

We froze the mixture the modern way, with a Donvier ice cream maker, and had excellent results. Perhaps our appetites are better; we feel this would serve six amply and would do for eight.

A Gracious Formal Dinner

Moving day was a gray, squally February morning when the Macdonalds left Leaskdale with all of their possessions crated and loaded into three horse-drawn cutters. Their destination was Norval, and the journey's uncertainties were somewhat discomfiting for Maud. They travelled by cutter to the train station at Uxbridge, where they and their belongings were transferred for the trip west. In Toronto they were met by Ernest and Ida Barraclough, members of the Union church in Ewan's new charge, who welcomed the Macdonalds and made every effort to ease their arrival. They dined at the Walker House Hotel near Toronto's Union Station, before setting out upon what was to be a long and troubled drive to the Barraclough's house in Glen Williams, a village just northwest of Norval. Maud found it an enormous relief to finally arrive, late at night, and be ushered in to the warmth and comfort of the Barraclough home. There they stayed for several days, with their hosts steering them through the church induction and helping to acquaint them with Norval before they began unpacking. The Barracloughs were pleasant folk and both Ewan and Maud found their conversation interesting; they became great friends

The Norval Presbyterian Church Manse.

and quickly abandoned their "minister and wife" role, which was otherwise important to maintain.

Ernest and Ida were regular dinner guests at the manse in Norval, but there were other formal callers in connection with Ewan's professional responsibilities, and supply ministers who took occasional services during Ewan's illness were asked to stay for dinner. Maud was a gracious hostess, offering excellent and generously portioned meals without a lot of fuss. She eschewed highly fashionable or stylish food for the quality of simpler fare. Many years earlier, Maud confided in her journal after a polite and tony luncheon had been given in her honour by her publisher's wife: "It was the 'smartest' function I attended in Boston. The menu was quite elaborate. Here it is – in memory of the first society function at which I was 'guest of honor'. Oyster cocktail, green turtle consomme, mushrooms under glass, devilled squab on toast, cucumber and tomato salad, with cheese balls, and ice cream. To tell the dreadful truth the only thing I really liked was the ice-cream. The other courses were very pretty but I wouldn't give a fig for them compared to a good P.E.I. 'duck supper' with accoutrements."

Maud's photograph of Norval's flour mill on the Credit River, the largest commercial enterprise in the village, until a devastating fire in 1930.

The recipes in this chapter are all "company" fare – the sorts of foods that would have been attractively presented to guests. They require a little more time to prepare than the dishes Maud and Ewan would have had at home alone. We have included Maud's Lemon Pie; it was her very favourite dessert and one in which she took great pride in serving!

A Gracious Formal Dinner

Menu

Pork Mock Duck with Apples and Stuffing
Southern Style Sweet Potatoes
Potato Puffs
Buttered Green Beans
Cranberry Jellied Salad

Red Currant Wine

Banana Cake with Nut Cream Filling

Alternatives

Fried Trout with Watercress
Lamb Chops with Pineapple
Asparagus with Lemon

Maud's Lemon Pie
New Moon Pudding

Frequently we find recipes from the 1920s and '30s which substitute a completely different ingredient for one which is temporarily unavailable. Maud's recipe book has several examples of such necessary accommodations; this is one, and she even has a second recipe for Mock Duck using round steak. Necessity certainly is the mother of invention!

Pork Mock Duck with Apples and Stuffing

Stuffing

3¼ c bread crumbs
¼ c finely choppped salt pork
1 onion *medium, finely chopped*
salt, pepper and savory to taste

Saute salt pork and onion together until onion is limp, add bread crumbs and seasonings. Moisten with a little water or chicken stock.

Mock Duck

2 large pork tenderloins
½ c strips of salt pork

Select two large pork tenderloins, split them open *horizontally from end to end leaving one side attached.* Flatten, *pound to form 2 rectangles.* Put dressing between the tenderloins and sew them together. *Skewers or toothpicks may be used for this.* Arrange strips of salt pork over the top. Place in a hot oven to sear then lower heat to bake. *Sear at 425°F for 10 minutes. Roast at 325°F for 25 to 30 minutes. When tenderloins are done* make gravy from fat in pan. *(See Roast Goose recipe in Chapter 8.)* *Serves six.*

Apples

4	apples
4 tsp	sugar
4 tbsp	butter

While tenderloins are cooking, prepare apples. Use large tart apples that will keep their shape. *(Northern Spies would be best.)* Pare, core, and quarter apples. Place them in a tightly covered saucepan with just a little water and set over fire *(medium heat)*. When they are tender arrange them in a covered baking dish, sprinkle lightly with sugar and generously with bits of butter – a tablespoon to each apple will be none too much. Cover dish and set it in oven where the apples may steam in the butter till they are very rich and almost transparent. Serve as a garnish around the "duck".

Sweet potatoes are a good accompaniment to pork and apples, and can be prepared well ahead of serving.

Southern Style Sweet Potatoes

6	sweet potatoes
8 tbsp	butter
3 tbsp	milk or cream
	salt and pepper
1	egg, well beaten

Select good sized evenly matched sweet potatoes. Scrub well and bake in a hot oven *(400°F)* until they are soft when squeezed. Cut in half lengthwise, scoop *out* and mash the potatoes and to each cupful add 1 tbsp butter, a very little milk or cream, salt and pepper. *Save the potato skins.* Fold in a well beaten egg.

Pack the mixture lightly into the potato shells, rounding the tops nicely. Brush over with soft butter. The mixture can be put in a baking dish if liked. Bake long enough to heat thoroughly and brown nicely on top. These can be prepared the day before and slipped into the oven for browning and reheating. *Serves six.*

This is a delicate presentation for the humble potato. A ricer is quite similar in structure to a garlic press but is much larger; cooked potatoes are forced through small holes, resulting in an even-textured "rice-like" consistency.

Potato Puffs

2 c	cooked riced potatoes *(pressed through a ricer or sieve)*
2 tbsp	butter
2	eggs, beaten
½ c	milk or cream
	salt and pepper

Stir butter into *warm* potatoes. Add eggs beaten till foamy, then milk *or cream.* Season to taste. Beat well and drop by spoonfuls 2 inches apart on greased pan. Bake in a quick oven *(450°F)* until *lightly* brown. *Watch closely.* Serve hot. *Serves six.*

Good with an added pinch of nutmeg.

Mixture may also be piped in large rosettes from a pastry bag onto greased cookie sheets. Brush the rosettes with a mixture of one beaten egg yolk and one tbsp water to ensure that they will brown nicely.

Buttered Green Beans

1 ½–2 lb	*green beans*
1 tbsp	*butter*

Remove stem end of beans. Leave whole or cut in pieces, depending on your preference. Pour boiling salted water over to barely cover and cook until crisp tender, about 10 minutes. Drain and toss with butter. Serves six.

This salad has a beautiful ruby red colour. We were tempted to keep the cranberries rather than discard them, but in Maud's day clear jellies were fashionable.

Cranberry Jellied Salad

2 c	cranberries
1 c	water
1 c	sugar
1 tbsp	gelatine
½ c	cold water
¼ tsp	salt
1 c	diced celery

Cook cranberries in 1 cup water until soft. Stir in sugar and cook for 5 minutes.

Soak gelatine in ½ c cold water for 5 minutes, then stir into hot cranberries until dissolved. Strain *and discard cranberries. Add salt to strained juice and chill.* When juice begins to thicken stir in celery, turn into a *square* wet pan and chill. When firm cut in squares, place a whole nut meat *(a pecan or walnut half)* on top of each square and serve on lettuce leaves with a garnish of mayonnaise. *Serves six.*

"I HAVE BEEN busy lately decanting 'home brew.' Last summer I made some red currant wine and some raspberry wine, from my recollection of Grandmother's method. Grandmother was famed for her currant wine. It *was* delicious – even Chateau Yquem was not much its superior. I was doubtful of my success for I was not sure I remembered her whole process and I knew of many folk who had followed her recipe straightly and produced but a sorry beverage. But either I had good luck or I have inherited some of her brain cells for my 'brew' is delicious – clear, ruby, sparkling with a quite sufficient 'bite'."

Red Currant Wine

9 quarts	fruit *(red currants)*
9 pints	water *(18 c)*
2 lb	sugar *(4 ½ c)*
1	*envelope dry yeast*
	additional sugar

Mash *fruit, water, 4 ½ c sugar and yeast together* and let stand 9 days, stirring every day. Drain *overnight* through jelly bag. *Measure juice.* To each *4 c of juice* add *an additional 2 ¼ c* sugar and let stand, covered, 9 days more *or until fermentation stops.* Filter *through fine cotton.* Put into *sterile* bottles. *Cork.* Keep in cool cellar. Don't use for a year.

Maud does not include yeast in her ingredient list. We feel it would be appropriate to add an envelope of dry yeast to the mashed fruit in order to avoid the development of undesirable yeast during the initial standing time.

An extravagant dessert like this is a grand finale to a special dinner. It deserves a more evocative title than Banana Cake, especially as the only bananas it contains are sliced and arranged on the top, with strawberries. Time consuming to make, but impressive to serve.

Banana Cake with Nut Cream Filling

3	egg yolks
1/4 c	cold water
1 1/2 c	sugar
1/2 tsp	lemon extract or grated rind of *one* lemon
1 c	*cake* flour sifted before measuring
1/4 c	cold water
1 c	*cake* flour
2 tsp	baking powder
1/2 tsp	salt
3	egg whites

(The two measures of flour and water are correct.)

Beat egg yolks. Then beat in each ingredient in order named, adding B.P. *(baking powder)* and salt with last cup of flour. Using a wooden spoon, fold in egg whites beaten very light. Bake in 2 greased layer pans at 350° F for about 20 minutes. Remove from pans while hot. When cold put together with nut cream filling.

Nut Cream Filling

3/4 c	sugar
1/3 c	*cake* flour
1/8 tsp	salt
1/2 c	walnuts or pecans chopped
2	eggs
2 c	scalded milk
1 tsp	vanilla
1 tsp	lemon flavouring

Mix dry ingredients. Add beaten eggs, then pour in the scalded milk. Cook in double boiler stirring constantly until mixture is thickened. Then cook for 10 minutes longer stirring occasionally. Remove from fire, cool and add flavouring. Place filling between layers with a thin coating of filling on top.

Topping

4	bananas
juice of	half a lemon
2 tbsp	powdered sugar
1 c	strawberries
1/2 c	sugar
2 c	whipped cream
1 tbsp	powdered sugar
1 tbsp	strawberry juice

Arrange on top 4 bananas sliced in rings. Sprinkle juice from half a lemon and about 2 tbsp powdered sugar over bananas. Then add 1 cupful of ripe strawberries after they have set awhile in 1/2 c sugar, or 1 cup strawberry jam. Cover the whole with a pint of whipped cream sweetened with 1 tbsp powdered sugar and 1 tbsp strawberry juice.

Indicative of her independent style, as a teen Maud fished with friends on Macneill's Pond, and always made a point of putting the worm on the hook herself. Unlike the other girls, she certainly didn't need any boy's help!

Fried Trout with Watercress

6	trout *about 8 oz each*
1 tbsp	bacon fat
1 tbsp	butter
1 tsp	salt

Split fish from head to vent, clean carefully but do not scrape flesh roughly. Leave head and tail on but remove gills and tongue. Wash in cold water and dry absolutely dry with clean cotton rags. Sprinkle a very little salt on the inside.

Put in frying pan a small amount of bacon grease and the same quantity of butter. Have grease very hot while carefully placing trout side by side in pan. Watch carefully that they don't burn. Turn but once. When one side is brown turn over with a griddle cake turner.

Serve on hot platter, the heads of each pair in opposite directions and have a border of watercress. Serve trout on hot plates with a sprig of cress.

Garnishes for Fish

Alternate slices of lemon and thinly sliced tomatoes, topped with a stuffed olive make a very gay garnish.

Lemon slices dipped in minced parsley alternated with slices of lemon dredged with paprika.

Thin slices of cucumber dipped in French dressing and sprinkled with parsley and paprika respectively. Arrange alternately in an overlapping circle around platter.

This recipe is fast and easy to prepare, leaving time to chat with guests before dinner.

Lamb Chops with Pineapple

3 lb	*1 inch thick lamb chops*
6	*pineapple rings*
1 tbsp	*butter*
	salt and pepper

Have butcher "French" the chops. Broil *3" under direct flame, 2 to 3 minutes per side.* Or pan broil until brown on both sides. Season with salt and pepper.

Fry pineapple slices in butter until throughly heated. Arrange chops and slices of pineapple alternately around the edge of the platter to form a ring. Fill the centre with buttered peas *or vegetables of your choice.* Garnish with sprigs of parsley. *Serves six.*

Maud served asparagus only in the spring, when the locally grown vegetable was at its best.

Asparagus with Lemon

2 lb	*asparagus*
2 tbsp	*butter, melted*
2 tbsp	*lemon juice*

Break off the tough lower stalks of the asparagus. Wash in cold water, tie in bunches with string, and stand upright in 2 inches of boiling salted water. Cover and cook just until tender. Lay on a warmed oval platter, snip string and pour over the asparagus a sauce made with the butter and lemon juice. Serves six.

Maud was rightly proud of her Lemon Pie, and while her recipe book contains other peoples' recipes for some variation of Lemon Pie, this is the one that gathered compliments, sometimes from unexpected sources!

"I AM KEEPING one eye on my writing and the other on the filling for my lemon pie. Which reminds me of a compliment I got last Sunday – an Englishman's compliment and such as only an Englishman could pay. We had Dr. Schofield supplying last Sunday – a medical missionary from Korea – a clever tactless man who certainly isn't afraid of man or devil. He seemed to have the Englishman's customary contempt of crude colonials, but when he had eaten his section of lemon pie at dinner he said 'Well, *at least*, you certainly do know how to make lemon pie.' The italics are mine! I remember that the only compliment Uncle Leander ever paid me in his life was to say that my lemon pies couldn't be beat. Who says that the way to a man's heart *isn't* through his stomach? I might have talked with the tongues of men and angels – I didn't – and it would not have extorted approval from Dr. Schofield. But the pie did the trick."

Maud's Lemon Pie

1 c	sugar
2 tbsp	cornstarch
	grated rind and juice of 1 lemon
1/8 tsp	salt
1	whole egg
2	egg yolks
1 c	water
2	egg whites
2 tbsp	sugar

Put an inch of water in the bottom of a double boiler and heat to simmer.

Into a bowl put the sugar and mix into it the cornstarch, grated lemon rind and juice, salt, one whole egg and the yolks of two. Mix well. Put 1 cup water in the top part of double boiler *over direct heat.* As soon as it boils stir in the sugar-lemon-egg mixture and place over simmering water. Cook until thick, about 15 minutes. Cool slightly and pour into baked crust.

Beat whites of eggs stiff with about 2 tbsp sugar and spread over pie. Brown slightly in oven. *425° F for 5 minutes.*

Maud wrote this recipe into her journal, and it was included in The Selected Journals of L.M. Montgomery *edited by Mary Rubio and Elizabeth Waterston. She was particularly fond of New Moon Pudding, and made it for special occasions. It is interesting to note that her recipe book gives twice the amount of sugar for the meringue that is found in the journal version. We have chosen the lesser amount, and have indicated a measurement for lemon juice. The original recipe in the cookbook makes a very large dessert. We have reduced it by half.*

New Moon Pudding

2 c milk
1 c breadcrumbs
1/3 c sugar
rind of 1/2 lemon
3 egg yolks, slightly beaten
1/4 tsp salt

3 egg whites
1/4 c sugar
1 1/2 tbsp lemon juice

Combine all ingredients and pour into a buttered 8x8x2 inch pan. Set into a larger pan and pour into the outer pan hot water to a depth of 1 inch. Bake in *a 350°F* oven until a silver knife *stuck into the center* comes out clean, *about 45 minutes.*

Beat whites of eggs stiff with sugar and lemon juice. Put on top *of pudding,* return to oven and *barely* brown *the meringue.* Serve cold with cream. *Serves six.*

The Work-a-Day World of a Minister's Wife

Montgomery's abundant energy was a blessing as she juggled keeping house, raising two boys, and attending to both her own career and Ewan's. In 1920, while Ewan ministered in Leaskdale, a typical December day began as follows: "Early rising per usual and Chester's lunch made ready. Then, with due housewifely care I took a batch of hams out of my pickle barrel and put a fresh batch in – neither a romantic nor a tragic proceeding. But I am fond of ham and one cannot live on tragedy and romance, so somebody must do the pickling." The next morning, after tidying the house, she made a crockful of brine for pickling tongues and, after a full day of writing and an evening out with the Guild, "I came home at 9:30 – and put a lot of old hens, which Lily had killed and dressed, into a tubful of salt and water to be ready for the next day's canning."

The old hens did indeed have her attention the following day. "Rise at 7:30. Chester's lunch and house as usual. Then Lily and I spent the forenoon cutting up the aforesaid hens and packing the pieces into glass sealers. After which I sorted out my linen closet, mended several things, made a saucepanful of cranberry sauce, and cleaned the fragments of meat off the boiled hen carcasses, out of which the fragments I concocted a very nice 'jellied chicken' mould for supper. I spent the afternoon in attending to the canning of the hens, thus transmogrifying them into 'canned chicken' – and I prepared all the ingredients necessary for a big fruit cake."

Maud was never without a housekeeper, but preferred, at times, to be involved with some of the bigger kitchen chores.

She also relished a few hours alone in the kitchen, making something special for the satisfaction of it. She found much of her hired help lacking in cooking ability, and set about training them as they arrived. Every woman has a particular way she prefers her kitchen run, and we suspect Maud's grumbles had more to do with having to train new staff in her ways than any lack of knowledge on their part. On Sunday evenings Maud made up a list of the upcoming week's chores and the menus to be prepared for each meal.

Maud's kitchen in the Norval Presbyterian Manse.

Ethel Dennis, a housekeeper in Norval, recalls that Montgomery bought the groceries, as a rule, and varied her meal plans so that something different was always served. As with all farming communities, the noon meal was called dinner and was more substantial than supper, which was served at the end of the day. Housekeepers always took their meals with the family, although when the boys weren't around supper could be a very quiet affair. When they were alone at the table, Maud often read and took notes through a meal, while Ewan played solitaire.

Upon the Macdonalds' arrival in Norval in February of 1926, Maud noted: "There was a general store, a hardware store, a bank, a butcher's shop – the usual equipment of the country village." Watson's Bakery was also in business, as were several blacksmith shops, a hotel, and a large flour mill owned by W.B. Browne. Unfortunately, none of these enterprises remain today, although the buildings that housed the bank, the general store, the hardware store and the bakery remain.

Even before the Macdonald family were completely settled in, Maud found there was much to like in her new home. "Norval manse is well designed and situated. It is of red brick. The kitchen is much larger and more convenient than the Leaskdale one. We have the soft water pump in the kitchen which is a good item, and there is a back staircase. . . . Our dining room here is large and light with a big bay window at the end and a door opening on to the verandah through which we can see the beautiful pine wood on the hill behind the village."

Maud's new electric range in her Norval kitchen.

The most significant change upon moving to Norval was the fact that the manse was electrically wired, and Maud had never lived anywhere so progressive. "I *do* like the electric light. It is an odd thing that last fall was the first time that I ever felt a longing for electric light. I had a gasoline lamp which I used for reading and sewing and I like it better than electric light. Do yet for that matter were it not for the trouble of fixing it up. And our flashlights were a great convenience. But all at once, last fall, long before I knew there was such a place as Norval I began to feel suddenly tired of coming in and fumbling in the dark for matches – tired of wrestling with wicks that no maid *ever* got straight. I felt that I'd like to have hydro. And here I have it. And after two weeks of it I wonder how I ever did without it! It gives me such a nice, omnipotent feeling to press a button – 'let there be light and there *is* light.'"

Electric power must have changed the routine of their daily living immeasurably. Maud embraced this time and effort saving development wholeheartedly. While her journal reflects a nostalgic preference for a good wood burning stove, there was not a moment's hesitation in selecting a new electric range when her old oil stove gave up the ghost. "We had an electric range installed today. The oil stove was done and since I had to get something I decided to get an electric range. I think I shall like it. It is clean and convenient. But if I had my choice of a cookery beast I'd choose an old 'Waterloo Stove' with plenty of good hardwood! It's odd to think we are cooking by the grace of that thunder of waters eighty miles away."

Maud also devoted considerable effort each winter to help with the production of the annual Old Timers' Concert. It was an evening of entertainment – song, recitations, and a play; those in the community who weren't taking part formed the audience. In 1927 Maud joined the group, reciting "The Widow Piper" while sporting a widow's dress and veil. Each year thereafter she helped organize the event, often directing the play. In November of 1930 she had already begun work for February's concert: "I have begun preparing a one act play for Old Tyme Night in February. Mr. Greenwood, Garfield McClure and his wife, and myself. So you will perceive it as an 'all star cast'. Mr. Greenwood, Anglican manager of the Bank of Nova Scotia here, is the best amateur actor I ever saw in my life. The play is the old one 'None so deaf as Those who won't Hear'.... It means work and time, of course, but somebody has to work to make that Old Tyme concert a success."

Doubtless, working on plays was considerably more fun than canning old hens. Even without her writing career, Maud's everyday life was chock-a-block full of myriad chores and interests. Our menu and selected alternatives are recipes that may be prepared ahead or in a hurry, and some use ingredients that could have been leftovers. Our generation is not the only one that has searched for fast easy meals!

The Work-a-Day World of a Minister's Wife

Menu

Swiss Potato Soup
Salmon Pie

Jellied Cucumber Salad
Baking Powder Biscuits

Apple Pie with Cheddar Cheese

Alternatives

Third Try Beef
Shepherd's Pie

Salmon and Cucumber Salad
Tomato Jelly Salad
Mrs. Fisher's Cornbread

Applesauce Cake
Boston Cookies

A smooth, flavourful soup that can be served warm or cold.

Swiss Potato Soup

4	*medium* potatoes
1	small white turnip
1	small onion
3 c	boiling water
4 c	hot milk
4 tbsp	butter
1/3 c	flour
1 1/2 tsp	salt
1/8 tsp	pepper

Wash potatoes, pare, cut in halves, and *peel and* slice the turnip. Parboil together 10 minutes and drain. *To the drained vegetables* add the sliced onion and 3 c boiling water.

Cook until vegetables are soft and drain, saving the water. Rub vegetables through a sieve *(or puree in an electric blender). Return vegetable puree to saucepan,* add *the saved* water and 4 cups hot milk.

In a small saucepan cook together the butter and flour. Add to soup *whisking until smooth.* Season with salt and pepper.

Serves six to eight, depending on portion size.

Salmon Pie

Other than the 1 lb can of salmon, Maud gives no specifics as to quantities, so we are presenting them to relieve guesswork. It is more a casserole than a pie, simple and quickly prepared.

1 lb	canned salmon
1/4 c	*thinly sliced raw* onion
4 c	*sliced cooked* potatoes
1 c	*white sauce (recipe given below)*

Shred the salmon, retaining juice. Place a layer of salmon in a buttered baking dish. On this place half the thinly sliced raw onions and on these half the sliced *cooked* potatoes. *Sprinkle with salt and pepper.* Repeat layers. *Salt and pepper the top layer of potatoes. Combine the white sauce with the reserved salmon juice and pour over the casserole. Sauce will be thin. Sprinkle with chopped parsley. Bake at 350°F for 20 minutes. Serves six.*

Standard White Sauce

2 tbsp	butter
1 tbsp	flour
1 c	milk
1/4 tsp	salt
dash	pepper

Melt butter slowly. Don't let it boil or bubble. Then remove from fire and add flour, salt and pepper. Mix until smooth. Add the milk and return to the heat. Stir and cook until thick enough.

This is a clear jelly with a delicate, refreshing flavour that accompanies cold meat or fish well. A few drops of green food colouring will brighten the colour.

Jellied Cucumber Salad

4 c	cucumbers, *peeled and* diced
1/2 tbsp	chopped onion
3 1/2 c	boiling water
1 tsp	salt
1/8 tsp	pepper
2 tbsp	vinegar
2 tbsp	granulated gelatin
1/4 c	cold water

Cook cucumber and onions in boiling water until cucumbers are tender. This takes about 20 minutes. Add salt, pepper, and vinegar. Remove from fire and add gelatine which has soaked for 5 minutes in the cold water. Stir until gelatine has dissolved. Press the mixture through a sieve and pour into individual moulds. Chill and serve with mayonnaise and cold meat. *Serves six.*

Finely chopped fresh dill and diced cucumber are nice additions to this jelly.

In this case, chill the jelly in a bowl until partially set, stir in 2 tbsp finely chopped dill and 1/2 c diced cucumber, then pour into individual moulds.

Best served hot from the oven, these biscuits fit any meal of the day. They can be split and served with butter and jam, accompany a salad or stew, or be rolled a bit thinner and used as a topping for Shepherd's Pie (later this chapter).

Baking Powder Biscuits

2 c	all purpose flour, sifted before measuring
4 tsp	baking powder
1 tsp	salt
2 tbsp	butter
2 tbsp	*shortening*
3/4 c	milk

Sift together the flour, baking powder, and salt. Rub into it, with a fork, the butter *and shortening. Still using a fork,* mix to a dough with 3/4 cup milk *plus one or 2 tbsp more milk as required to clear the bowl.* Toss on floured board and roll lightly to 1 inch thick.

Cut *with a floured two-inch cutter.* Place on *ungreased* pan and bake in a hot oven *(450°F)* for 12 to 15 minutes.

Serve hot. Makes a dozen 2-inch biscuits.

Maud has the shortest of recipes for apple pie, so we've followed it with the recipe we use at Crawford's. Our customers have been telling us that we make the best apple pie around, and we'd like to share ours with you!

Apple Pie

Pare and cut apples in thin slices. Sprinkle with sugar (1 tbsp to 1 apple) and nutmeg and dot with butter. Mix 1/4 tsp salt with sugar. Bake till apples are tender.

Crawford's Apple Pie

4 1/2–5 c	*thinly sliced apples*
2/3–3/4 c	*sugar, depending on tartness of apples*
1 tsp	*commercial instant starch (you can substitute 1 tbsp flour)*
1/2 tsp	*cinnamon*
pinch	*nutmeg*
pinch	*salt*

Toss the apples in the combined sugar, flour, and spices. Pile into the pie shell, settling the slices as compactly as possible. Moisten the edge of the crust with water. Lay the top crust over and flute the edges together. Make small slits in the top crust to allow steam to escape. Bake at 425°F for about 12 minutes, then reduce heat to 375°F for 30 minutes, or until the apples do not resist a sharp knife.

At Crawford's the first fall apples we use in our pies are Wealthys. They are great tart apples, cook quickly and require watching as they near doneness (apples will explode through the top crust if slightly overdone). Later-ripening Northern Spys are our mainstay from mid-October on to June, when apple storages are empty. Spys take longer to cook, but keep their shape nicely; their tart flavour makes for an excellent apple pie. We use apples grown in Norval and are lucky to be surrounded by one of the best apple growing areas in Ontario.

We serve Old Ontario Cheddar Cheese with apple pie, preferably a raw milk cheddar. As everyone knows, apple pie without cheese is like a kiss without a squeeze!

Maud's Pie Crust

2 c	pastry flour, measured before sifting
1/4 tsp	salt
1/4 tsp	baking powder
1 c	lard, crisco, bacon fat or pork fat

Using a fork rub lard into flour until it is like small peas. Add sufficient ice cold water to handle. This makes two crusts. *(One double crust or two single shells)*

Pastry Hints

1) Mix quickly and lightly.
2) Sprinkle water on a little at a time, just enough to hold pastry together.
3) Have everything as cold as possible.
4) Bake in a quick oven.
5) Never grease pie plates.
6) For a shell, prick rolled pastry well before taking it from board instead of after it is in pan.

A Note From Crawford's:
Present day cooks would be shocked at the free use of animal fats in many old recipes. Although we concur that lard makes a good pastry, being flakier and better flavoured, we satisfy our customers' expectations by using vegetable shortening and unbleached flour in our pastry.
We can verify Maud's hints by saying that handling is all important. Let pastry rest at least 15 minutes before rolling out, roll it on a board lightly dusted with bread flour to prevent sticking, ease it into the pie plate, never stretch it. Pie shells need be pricked only if they are to contain custard or cream fillings, in which case they must rest, preferably overnight, before baking.

You've had it as Roast Beef. The next day you've sliced it for sandwiches. What to do when its still not finished?

Third Try Beef

3 c	cold roast beef cut in neat little cubes
½	of a Spanish onion cut very fine
2 tbsp	beef drippings and
2 tbsp	browned flour
1	Oxo or Beefex cube or 1 tsp Bovril *(or any instant beef bouillon)*
2 c	boiling water
6	carrots
1 lb	fresh peas or a tin

Cut carrots into four lengthwise pieces and put them to cook in boiling salted water.

Fry onion in dripping till light brown and add browned flour and water. Add beef cube, salt, and pepper *to taste* and finally meat. *Stir and simmer while it thickens.*

When it is brown turn out on platter and surround with peas and carrots. *Serves six.*

Another way of using up leftover roast beef. Leftover mashed potatoes can replace the sliced potatoes if you're trying to clean out the fridge!

Shepherd's Pie

3 c	*beef*
2 tbsp	*bacon fat*
½	onion
½	*stalk* celery
	boiling water
2 tbsp	flour
½ c	cold water
4 c	potatoes, cooked and sliced

Cut cold meat *(beef)* in ½ inch cubes *and brown in bacon fat.* Add half an onion and a bit of celery, *both chopped fine.* Cover with boiling water and cook slowly about one hour. Thicken the water with flour and cold water *mixed smoothly together.*

Put a layer of cold sliced *cooked* potato in bottom of *a 10-cup casserole* pan, put meat on this and pour the gravy over it. Finish with a layer of potatoes. Bake till hot *at 400°F.* In place of top layer of potatoes meat may be covered with baking powder biscuit dough *(see recipe this chapter)* and baked till dough is done *at 450°F for about 15 minutes.* Serves six.

A simple, make-ahead salad for a busy day. Dried elbow macaroni was commonly available in the 1920s and was used in casseroles and salads. Other pasta shapes had not reached any popularity at that point.

Salmon and Cucumber Salad

1 lb	canned salmon
2 ½ c	cold cooked macaroni
2	medium sized cucumbers, chopped
½ c	mayonnaise
1 tsp	salt
6	*lettuce leaves*
1	*lemon*

Mix ingredients and let stand in ice box 2 or 3 hours before serving. Arrange on crisp lettuce leaves. Garnish with slices of cucumber, lemon, and a spoonful of mayonnaise.

A little lemon juice squeezed over salad just before garnishing is nice. Serves six.

This salad goes nicely with Shepherd's Pie. We like to substitute vegetable cocktail for tomato juice for a little extra zestiness.

Tomato Jelly Salad

2 c	tomato juice *(we recommend vegetable cocktail)*
2 tbsp	mild *(white)* vinegar
1 tsp	sugar
bit of	bay leaf
1 slice	onion
1 tbsp	lemon juice
2 tbsp	gelatine
½ c	cold water
	green peas or finely chopped cabbage

Heat tomato juice to the boiling point with seasonings. *Remove from heat.*

Stir in gelatine which has been soaked 5 minutes in ½ c cold water. Strain mixture into moulds, let stand until cool and beginning to set. Add 2 tsp vegetable to each, mix gently and set in a cool place to chill. When firm unmould on nest of lettuce leaves. Pass dressing separately. *Fills 6 half-cup molds. Serves six.*

Mrs. Fisher was on staff at Macdonald College in Montreal, where Frede Campbell, Maud's cousin and confidante, studied. Maud visited Frede often, and this recipe may have been served at one of the luncheons that Mrs. Fisher gave.

Mrs. Fisher's Cornbread

1 ½ c	cornmeal
½ c	sugar
½ tsp	salt
2 tbsp	butter
½ c	boiling water
2	egg yolks, beaten
½ c	milk
1 c	flour, spooned into cup
4 tsp	baking powder
2	egg whites, stiffly beaten

Measure first 4 ingredients into a bowl. Stir in the boiling water. Allow to cool.

Then add the beaten egg yolks and the milk. Sift the flour and baking powder together and beat in. Fold in carefully the 2 stiffly beaten egg whites.

Bake in a greased *8x8x2 inch* cake tin or muffin pans in a *375°F* oven for 30 minutes.

This interesting recipe appears in Maud's book with no eggs and the advice to "turn into a greased loaf pan lined with greased white paper." *It is a dense, heavy cake and certainly needs a larger pan than our conventional 9x5x3 loaf pan. We add 2 eggs and recommend a different pan. The old fashioned seeded raisins or "sticky" raisins, as they used to be called, contribute to this cake's wonderful flavour.*

Applesauce Cake

1 c	white sugar
¾ c	melted butter
2	*eggs*
1 ½ c	applesauce
2 c	flour
1 tsp	soda
½ tsp	baking powder
¼ tsp	salt
1 ½ tsp	cinnamon
½ tsp	nutmeg
⅓ tsp	ground cloves
1 c	seeded and cut raisins
1 c	dates, chopped
½ c	walnuts, chopped

Beat sugar and melted butter together well. Beat in eggs and then applesauce.

Mix and sift dry ingredients. Mix fruit and sprinkle well with flour mixture. Then add all the rest of the dry mixture *to the fruit* and when thoroughly combined add *to the applesauce mixture.* Beat well for 2 minutes.

Line the bottom of a 2-part 9-inch tube pan with paper, cut to fit. Grease the sides and bottom. Turn batter into pan.

Bake in oven at 350°F for 50 to 60 minutes or until cake shrinks from side of pan.

This will keep 2 weeks.

One of Maud's housekeepers commented that she was frequently requested to make Boston Cookies. The Macdonald family's cookie jar simply kept emptying!

Boston Cookies

1 c	butter
1 ½ c	brown sugar
3	eggs, well beaten
1 tsp	*baking* soda
1 ½ tbsp	hot water
3 ¼ c	bread flour sifted before measuring
½ tsp	salt
1 tsp	cinnamon
1 c	chopped walnuts
1 c	chopped raisins

Cream butter, add sugar gradually, then the eggs well beaten. Add soda dissolved in hot water and half the flour sifted with the salt and cinnamon. Then add nuts & fruit well mixed in remaining flour. Drop by dessertspoonfuls *(tablespoons)* one inch apart on buttered tins *(cookie trays)* and bake in moderate oven. *350°F for 12 to 14 minutes. Yield five dozen.*

Summer Lunch and Picnic Fare

Summer was a particularly social season with good weather bringing a raft of picnics, garden parties, and lawn socials. Norval Presbyterian Church held an annual garden party on the manse lawn, an event so well attended that all of the pews were removed from the church and rowed up on the lawn for the day's entertainment program. In her journal, Maud describes a stage as being built "on and from" the manse verandah, and relates the blur of activity: "I rose at six and made cake, candy etc. All day and all night I nearly ran my feet off. There were a thousand people on the grounds and the house was over-run with the performers, and somebody wanting something every minute."

Marion, Keith, and Ernest Webb with Chester Macdonald during an afternoon at Cavendish beach, 1919.

A week later Maud took sandwiches to the Norval Presbyterian Women's Auxiliary picnic, which followed the group's monthly meeting and address, and the very next day she attended Union Presbyterian's Missionary Picnic, where she "ate the most delicious strawberry short-cake I ever tasted. It would praise its maker in the gates." Church social activities didn't end with the two churches in Ewan's charge; in August of 1926

Maud was giving readings at a lawn social in Georgetown, "Because we want the Georgetown people to come back and help *us* in our programs."

Sometimes Sunday School Picnics were held in pretty places far removed from the village of Norval, and people made a day's outing of the event. Marion Laird recalls everyone climbing into cars and travelling to Lasalle Park in Burlington for a picnic, and also to Stanley Park in Erin. Ewan and Maud drove a Wyllis Knight, a car that "always started up with a huge cloud of smoke," according to long-time Norval resident Lloyd Hustler. Of course, lots of cooking goes along with frequent get-togethers. For the Sunday School Picnic at Stanley Park, Maud recounts making a jelly roll, cherry pies, tarts, cookies, date loaf, sandwiches and lemonade. Quite a significant contribution from a busy author!

The Webb girls picnicing with friends on the red rocks of Cavendish beach.

Maud must have loved the quiet beauty of her own back yard in the summer too, without the crowds of all these celebrations. Perhaps she and Ewan and the boys sat out in the shade of a big maple with the Credit River flowing lazily by, and had little picnics all by themselves. They might have enjoyed any of the light, easy foods that we give recipes for in this chapter.

Summer Lunch and Picnic Fare

Menu

Chicken Mould

Watermelon Rind Pickles

Potato Salad with O.A.C. Dressing

Sunshine Salad

Frede's Muffins

Pink Lemonade

Fruit Punch

Cream Caramel Cake

Lemon Crumbles

Alternatives

Mock Chicken

Salmon Mould

Butterscotch Squares

Here is Maud's recipe for a cold, summertime dish using up leftovers from a cooked chicken.

Chicken Mould

Clean scraps off carcass and run them through chopper. For every 7 cups ground meat use 3 ½ tsps salt, some pepper and onion. Dissolve a box of Knox gelatin in cold water or water from bones. Thin enough to mix well with meat. Pack meat in mould and set away under weight.

You'll find it much easier to follow our more detailed version, given below. Use a food processor to grind the chicken.

3 ½ c	*ground chicken*
1 tbsp	*finely chopped onion*
1 ½ tsp	*Knox gelatin (or other unflavoured gelatin)*
¼ c	*cold water*
¾ c	*stock from roasted chicken*
1 ½ tsp	*salt*
¼ tsp	*pepper*

Soften the gelatin in the cold water. Heat the stock, add the salt and pepper and stir in the softened gelatin until dissolved. Add the stock mixture to chicken and onion.

Mix well and turn into mould or bowl with a weighted saucer on top. Refrigerate.

This has a fine texture and slices nicely. Serve on salad plates. Serves six.

These days many folks are no longer familiar with Watermelon Rind Pickles, but they're tasty and have a pretty, translucent appearance made even more attractive if you leave a little of the pink flesh on the rind.

Watermelon Rind Pickles

	rind of large watermelon, cut in oblong pieces
	iced water
3 tbsp	alum
2 tbsp	ground cinnamon
2 tbsp	ground cloves
2 tbsp	ground ginger
5 lb	brown sugar
4 c	vinegar

Cut rind of large watermelon in oblong pieces. *Set in large pot and* cover with iced water. Add alum. Soak overnight. Drain. Cover with fresh water. Boil 1 hour. Drain.

Tie 2 tbsp each cinnamon, cloves and ginger (all ground) in a *fine net* bag. Bring brown sugar to boil with vinegar with bag in it. Add rind and cook an hour or till quite tender.

Set in cellar overnight. Boil 15 minutes and bottle *in sterilized jars.*

With the high ratio of other vegetables and eggs to potatoes, this could be considered a main course salad.

Potato Salad with O.A.C. Dressing

2 c	cold cooked potatoes, sliced
4	hard-boiled eggs *finely chopped*
1 c	cold cooked peas
1	green pepper *finely diced*
2	small onions *finely chopped*

Mix above ingredients thoroughly with O.A.C. dressing.

Serve on lettuce. Garnish with slices of egg and tomato.

O.A.C. Dressing

This recipe comes from Frede Campbell, who took a short food science course at the Ontario Agricultural College (O.A.C., now the University of Guelph), and came away with this recipe. Maud liked to take the radial train from Norval to Guelph, to visit the college's extensive greenhouses.

3/4 c	sugar
2 tbsp	flour
1 tsp	salt
2 tsp	mustard *powder*
2 c	milk
4	eggs, beaten
2 tbsp	butter, melted
1 c	*white* vinegar

Mix dry ingredients together *(in top of a double boiler)*, add beaten eggs, then melted butter and milk. Stir *over simmering water* in double boiler *for about 15 minutes. When it starts to thicken* add vinegar very gradually. Keep on stirring until it thickens so as to prevent curdling. This makes a large amount. Halve it for ordinary occasions. Equal quantities of this dressing and whipped cream combined make a nice dressing for all kinds of salads.

Makes 3 1/3 c of dressing, which keeps very well in the refrigerator. The whipped cream is not a necessary addition.

Fruity, festive and colourful – a good picnic salad.

Sunshine Salad

1 tbsp	gelatine
1/4 c	cold water
1 c	pineapple juice
1/4 c	vinegar
1/4 tsp	salt
1/2 c	orange juice, strained
1/4 c	white vinegar
1 c	orange pieces
1 1/2 c	cooked *(canned)* pineapple, cut in small cubes
1 c	raw young carrot, grated or chopped fine
	lettuce
	mayonnaise

Soften gelatine in cold water for 5 minutes. Heat the pineapple juice and add it, and stir until the gelatine is dissolved. Combine with orange juice and vinegar. Cool and set in ice box to chill. When mixture begins to set add orange, pineapple and carrot. Chill in one large mould or individuals. When firm serve on lettuce with dressing *(mayonnaise).*

Frede Campbell, Maud's close friend and cousin, graduated in Household Science from Macdonald College in Montreal. Maud describes her own recipe book as being "full of the Macdonald College recipes she gave me," and this is one. Muffins were often called gems and the pans in which they were baked were known as gem pans. These muffins are good served with your favourite jam.

Frede's Muffins

3 tbsp	butter or roast pork fat or bacon fat
3 tbsp	white sugar
1	egg
½ c	milk
1 c	*all purpose* flour
2 tsp	baking powder
½ tsp	salt

Beat the butter and sugar together, then beat in the egg. Add the milk alternately with the sifted dry ingredients, beating lightly. Bake in *greased* gem pans *(muffins pans, filled ⅔ full) at 400°F for 20 to 25 minutes.* Makes 6 large muffins or 8 small ones. *Serve warm.*

Mix just before serving and there will be a frothy pink topping on every glass!

Pink Lemonade

1 ½ c	red jelly (sour cherry, currant, or any other desired flavour)
1 c	sugar
2 ½ c	lemon juice
2 c	water
6 c	*additional* water

Combine first four items. Beat well with a rotary egg beater *or electric blender.* Add *additional* water and pour over ice cubes or cracked ice. Serve in tall glasses. Serves 12.

A big punch bowl on a picnic table adds elegance to the occasion. The juice mixture can be prepared in advance and carried to the picnic site in jars, ready for assembling with ice and water or gingerale.

Fruit Punch

12	oranges
6	lemons
1 c	canned pineapple juice
½ c	maraschino cherries
2 c	water
	sugar
8 c	water or gingerale

Squeeze oranges and four of the lemons. Slice the other two. Add pineapple juice to orange and lemon juice.

Cut orange and lemon rinds into strips *and place in medium saucepan.* Add 2 cups of water and sweeten to taste. Boil until *rind strips are* tender, *discard rinds and add cooking water to fruit juice.* Add *up to 8 cups* water or gingerale to the fruit juice. Pour over blocks of ice, garnish with cherries *and lemon slices* and serve in a large punch bowl. This recipe serves about 12.

This is a one-layer cake that cuts easily into squares and does not need to be served on a plate.

Cream Caramel Cake

2	eggs
7/8 c	brown sugar
3/4 c	thick cream
1 2/3 c	*all purpose* flour
2 1/2 tsp	baking powder
1/2 tsp	salt
1 tsp	cocoa

Beat eggs, brown sugar and cream together until the mixture is somewhat thickened.

Sift the flour, baking powder and salt together, add the cocoa and beat all together thoroughly. Pour into a square *8x8x2 inch* pan lined with buttered paper *(waxed paper)* and bake in a moderate oven. *350°F for 25 to 30 minutes.*

Caramel Icing

3 c	brown sugar
1 1/2 tsp	cornstarch
1/2 c	milk
1/8 tsp	salt
2 tbsp	butter
1 tsp	vanilla

Cook sugar, cornstarch, milk and salt together and stir until lumps are entirely dissolved. Continue stirring through boiling. Boil to soft ball *stage (when a few drops of hot sugar mixture, dropped into a cup of cold water, can be gathered into a soft ball with your finger tip).* Remove from fire, add butter and let get quite cool before adding vanilla. Beat vigorously until it holds its shape on cake. One cup chopped nuts may be added.

Buttery and rich with just the right amount of lemon, these squares must have been a favourite with Maud, who was quite partial to the flavour of lemon.

Lemon Crumbles

First prepare the filling:

1 c	sugar
1 tbsp	flour
¾ c	water
1	egg, slightly beaten
1	lemon – grated rind and juice

In a saucepan mix sugar and flour and stir in water and slightly beaten egg. Cook, stirring constantly until smoothly thickened. Remove from heat and add lemon rind and juice. Cool *while mixing the following as a base and top:*

¾ c	*all purpose* flour
1 tsp	baking powder
¾ c	butter
½ c	white sugar
1 c	*medium flaked* coconut
1 ½ c	cracker crumbs *(regular soda crackers)*

Sift flour and baking powder together. Mix in butter. Then add sugar, coconut and cracker crumbs. Spread ½ this mixture in a buttered *9x9 inch* baking tin *and press firmly*. Add filling, then spread balance of mixture on top. Bake in a moderate oven until nicely browned. *350°F for 25 minutes. Cut in small squares when cool.*

Mock chicken appears frequently in Maud's journals as she rhymes off the list of dishes she has prepared for innumerable church socials, luncheons, and picnics.

Mock Chicken

2 lb	lean fresh pork *cut in 2-inch pieces*
2	small carrots, sliced
	outside stalks and leaves of 2 bunches of celery
1	onion *cut in quarters*
1 or 2	bay leaves
2 tsp	salt
1/2 tsp	pepper
1	envelope Knox gelatine *(or any unflavoured gelatine)*

Add all ingredients except the gelatine to a large saucepan, cover with water and cook till done *(simmer for one hour or more). Remove meat from stock. Strain stock, discard vegetables.* Run meat through food chopper, *or use food processor to shred fine.*

Dissolve 1 envelope of Knox gelatine *in 1/2 c of the stock. Mix into the ground pork,* then add enough of the strained stock to moisten meat well. Pack in mould *or 9x5x3 inch loaf pan. Refrigerate under weight. Serves six.*

Choose red salmon for this mould, as it looks so vibrant and pretty on a frilly green lettuce leaf.

Salmon Mould

1 lb	canned salmon
½ tbsp	salt
1 ½ tbsp	sugar
½ tbsp	flour
1 tsp	mustard *powder*
dash	cayenne
2	egg yolks, slightly beaten
1 ½ tbsp	butter, melted
¾ c	milk
¼ c	vinegar *or lemon juice*
1 tbsp	gelatine
2 tbsp	cold water

Mix salmon with salt, sugar, flour and cayenne. Then add the egg yolks, melted butter, milk and vinegar. Cook in double boiler until mixture thickens. Soak gelatine in cold water and add to salmon. Turn into individual moulds *that have been greased with vegetable oil.* Let harden *refrigerated* all night.

Serves six people. Goes well with potato salad. *Garnish with snipped chives.*

An easy to make square, dense and chewy.

Butterscotch Squares

1/4 c	butter
1 c	brown sugar
1	egg
3/4 c	flour
1 tsp	baking powder
1/4 tsp	salt
1 1/2 tsp	vanilla
1/4 c	nut meats

Cook butter and sugar, *stirring* till well blended. Cool to lukewarm. Add unbeaten egg and beat well. Sift flour with baking powder and salt *and add to mixture.* Then add vanilla and nuts. Spread like fudge in *greased 8-inch square* pan. Bake in moderate oven *(350°F)* 25 minutes. *Do not overbake.* Cut in squares. *Dust with confectioner's sugar.*

Old Friends Come to the Table

Some of Maud's dearest friendships were forged early in life, mostly on Prince Edward Island. Although Maud was always outgoing and sociable, there were a few she held closer than the rest, recognizing instantly a kinship of thought, sensitivity, and appreciation. At the age of fifteen, one of her best school chums was Nathan Lockhart, the Baptist minister's step-son, who read as voraciously as Maud and loved to talk about the books they had exchanged. At that time, Maud found no one else in Cavendish as interested in intellectual dialogue. During the year that Maud spent with her father in Prince Albert, Saskatchewan, she became close friends with Laura and Will Pritchard, a brother and sister pair who shared her sense of humour and were always ready to join her headstrong pursuit of fun. And Frede Campbell, her Park Corner cousin, was perhaps her best-loved and trusted confidante, close in nature and completely understood.

Maud in her flower garden at the Norval Presbyterian Manse.

Nora Lefurgey was an old Island friend too, a school teacher in Cavendish who shared Maud's delight in "our wild exultant dips in stormy waves – our walks together over shadowy hills – all the fool things we did for the fun of doing them." They met as young women and their friendship was immediate. For a while they pursued authorship of a cooperative diary, with Maud writing one day and Nora the next, creating a humourous record of their antics and jokes. "Ridiculous" fun, as Maud noted.

Both women married and left the Island, their lives unfolding in different directions. While Ewan and Maud were living in Leaskdale, Nora wrote from British Columbia, where she lived with her husband, Edmond Campbell, and their sons. But by the time the Macdonalds moved to Norval, Maud had completely lost touch with her old friend.

Myrtle Webb during a visit to Maud at the Norval Prebyterian Manse, 1926.

Imagine her delight several years later when Nora suddenly appeared in Toronto, where they had moved for their sons to attend Upper Canada College. Their friendship rekindled instantly, despite the passing of twenty-four years since they had last been together. Nora and Edmond (Ebbie, as he was affectionately known) came out to Norval to spend a week at the manse in the summer of 1932. In her journal, Maud recounts: "Nora and I drove and made strawberry jam and went for long delightful walks together and talked. Oh, how we talked and how good it was! One afternoon we went up to the Y Camp and came home through the woods along the West Branch of the Credit. We picked and ate wild strawberries for an hour. I had never seen a wild berry since we came to Norval. We found a corner full of wild honeysuckle – we saw three cute baby skunks – saw them only! – we told stories and ragged each other and shrieked with laughter. This seemed good to me. I thought I had forgotten how to laugh – really laugh."

The menu we suggest could have been served during that happy week; comfortable, flavourful stews and roasts, favourite desserts, and, of course, a celebratory glass or two of Dandelion Wine.

Old Friends Come to the Table

MENU

Lamb Stew with Browned Potatoes

Glazed Carrots

Minted Peas

Dandelion Wine

Mrs. B's Rice Pudding

Orange Cookies

ALTERNATIVES

German Pot Roast

Casserole Chicken

Lettuce Salad with French Dressing

Pickled Beets

Nora's Pudding

Mock Cherry Pie

There is something comfortable and homey about a slowly simmered stew, in spite of its humble ingredients.

Lamb Stew

2 lb	lean raw lamb (breast, shoulder, neck, flank, and trimmings are all good for lamb stew)
1/4 c	flour, mixed with 1 tsp salt and 1/2 tsp pepper
2 tbsp	butter
1/2 c	onion, sliced
3 c	turnip, diced
1	green pepper, chopped
3 c	water

Wipe meat with a damp cloth, cut into small pieces and roll in flour *seasoned with salt and pepper.* Melt the butter in a skillet, add the onions and cook until they turn yellow. Add the meat. When meat and onion have browned delicately, transfer them to a deep kettle.

Add water to the skillet and stir to get the full benefit of browned bits left in skillet. *Add to meat in kettle.* Cover and simmer for one hour.

Add turnip, green pepper and *your choice of* seasonings *to taste,* and cook 30 minutes longer. *Add more water if necessary.* If stew is not thick enough, add 1 tbsp flour mixed with 2 tbsp cold water and cook for several minutes longer, stirring constantly. Serve hot with browned potatoes. *Serves six.*

Browned Potatoes

Heat bacon drippings or butter in a frying pan. Season peeled, sliced, cooked potatoes with salt. Add to frying pan. Allow to become golden before turning.

This is the recipe for Stuart's much-loved "candied carrots."

Glazed Carrots

12	medium carrots, sliced on the diagonal, boiled until just tender
½ c	granulated sugar
¼ c	water
4 tbsp	butter
2 tbsp	chopped parsley

Dissolve sugar in water and add to butter in a cold frying pan. Heat until butter melts. Add carrots and parsley and heat until carrots are glazed but not brown. *Serves six.*

Maud doesn't have a recipe for Minted Peas in her ledger, but we feel the flavour combination with lamb is so nice that we're suggesting a simple recipe. She may have done this herself, and not bothered to write it down.

Minted Peas

3 c	*fresh or frozen peas*
4	*6-inch sprigs of fresh mint*
½ tsp	*salt*

Pour boiling water over the peas and mint just to cover. Return to the boil and boil only one minute for frozen peas, five minutes for fresh. Discard mint. Serves six.

"WHAT DO I like?... I like pretty china and glass and old heirloom things... I like doing fancy work and I like cooking and I like eating the nice things that other people cook... I like open fires and moonlit nights... I like a snack at bed time. I like spruce gum... I like chocolate caramels and Brazil nuts. I like – or liked in pre-prohibition days – Miss Oxtoby's dandelion wine."

Miss Mary Oxtoby and her sister Lizzie had a farm behind the Macdonald's manse in Leaskdale. Upon their arrival, Ewan and Maud boarded with the two spinsters "who would have delighted Dickens," *until the manse was made ready. Maud found an* "innocent sweetness" *about Mary, whose recipe for Dandelion Wine follows.*

Dandelion Wine

2 quarts	dandelion flowers
2	lemons
3 lb	sugar
1	yeast cake *(or one packet dry yeast)*

Boil dandelions in four quarts of water for 3 minutes. Strain and discard dandelions. Add the lemons, cut up, and the sugar. Put on the fire again and boil for 3 minutes. Remove from heat and cool.

When cold put in a half slice of toast with a yeast cake spread over it. *If using dry yeast, stir into liquid.* Let it stand until it stops singing, *at least overnight, loosely covered.* Filter and cork air tight.

Ernest and Ida Barraclough made their home in Glen Williams, where Ernest was the general manager of the Glen Woollen Mill. They enjoyed the Macdonalds' company, and their home quickly became a haven of sorts, where both Ewan and Maud felt comfortable to converse freely. "Mrs. B." was an excellent cook in Maud's estimation, and the Macdonalds spent many an evening having supper in the Glen with their new friends. This is Mrs. B's recipe for a comforting rice pudding.

Mrs. B's Rice Pudding

½ c	long grain rice
2 c	milk
½ tsp	salt

Stir rice, milk and salt in a buttered baking dish. Cover and bake in a *250°F* oven for two hours, stirring occasionally. Refrigerate overnight.

To the cooked rice add:

1 c	milk
2	eggs, beaten
½ c	white sugar
½ tsp	salt
½ tsp	grated lemon rind
½ tsp	vanilla
½ tsp	nutmeg

Stir gently into the cooked rice. Place 1 tsp butter on top. Cover and bake *at 300°F* until barely set, about 30 minutes. Pudding will thicken after standing. Serve with cream.
Serves eight.

This is one of those recipes that calls for "juice of one orange" *and* "flour to make a soft dough." *For clarity we've specified the amounts of both juice and flour. This soft cookie can be made a little fancier with a dab of Orange Icing (see recipe for Park Corner Ribbon Cake in Chapter Six) on top of each cookie.*

Orange Cookies

1 c	brown sugar
½ c	shortening *or butter*
⅓ c	orange juice
	grated rind of one orange
1	egg
¼ tsp	salt
1 tsp	vanilla
2 tsp	cream of tartar
1 tsp	*baking* soda
2 c	flour

Cream butter and sugar, then add juice and rind of orange. Beat egg lightly and add it.

Mix *baking* soda and cream of tartar with a little flour and sift it in. Add flour to make a soft dough that will roll. Mix cookies before turning on oven. Let them stand while oven is heating. *Chilling the dough for ten minutes makes it easier to roll.* Roll out a small portion at a time *on a floured board.* Cut with an oblong cutter, mark *a design* lightly across the top of each and bake *on a greased cookie sheet* in a moderate oven. *350°F for 10 to 12 minutes. Yields approximately 4 dozen fingers.*

Alternatively, spoonfuls of dough may be rolled into 1-inch balls, flattened slightly and baked in the same manner.

Be sure to start marinating the roast the day before you plan to serve it. This advance preparation and the long slow cooking time not only gives the roast a wonderful flavour but also allow lots of time to prepare the rest of the meal and socialize with your friends as well. Leftovers make great sandwiches.

German Pot Roast

4 lb	beef rump roast (or other suitable cut)
½ tsp	ground nutmeg
½ tsp	cinnamon
¼ tsp	cloves
1	medium onion
1	bay leaf
½ c	vinegar
½ c	brown sugar
1 c	carrots, diced
1 c	celery, chopped

Mix spices together and rub them into sides of roast. Slice the onion and put it and the bay leaf in a large bowl and lay the meat on top. Mix the vinegar and sugar together and pour over the whole. Let stand in refrigerator overnight or until ready to use the next day.

When ready to cook, remove meat from marinade, pat dry, brown in a little oil in a hot frying pan. Place in a large casserole. Add vinegar and sugar mixture and about 1 cup of water. Bake slowly in *a 300°F* oven about 4 hours. Add the carrots and celery and bake one more hour.

To Make Gravy

Remove meat and vegetables and keep them warm. Whisk ¼ c flour into ½ c water, stir into stock in casserole and simmer about 5 minutes, stirring frequently.

Slice the meat. Present on platter ringed with the celery, carrots, and onion. Pass the gravy separately. Mashed potatoes or buttered noodles would be appropriate.

Accompany with green peas or beans. Serves eight generously, with leftovers for sandwiches.

Maud would have purchased a whole chicken from her butcher or local farmer, but nowadays chicken pieces are conveniently available for a casserole such as this.

Casserole Chicken

1	chicken or hen, cut up *(4-5 lb)*
6	small onions
1	small bunch celery, diced
1	green pepper, diced
	salt and pepper
1 or 2 c	canned or green *(fresh)* peas

Brush chicken over with melted fat. Put it and diced vegetables in a casserole. *You may leave the onions whole.* Cook uncovered in a hot oven till brown. Then cover chicken with hot water or broth, season with salt and pepper *and ½ tsp dried thyme or 2 fresh sprigs.* Cook until tender *in a 350°F oven for 45 to 60 minutes. A stewing hen may require 2 hours.* Add peas half an hour before serving. Thicken liquid with a little flour. *(2 tbsp mixed in ¼ c cold water, stirred into bubbling liquid.) Serves six.*

If for supper, serve with Baking Powder Biscuits. *(see Chapter 3)*

Crunchy green salads abundantly full of different vegetables were not in vogue in Maud's day. You may find this salad somewhat restrained, but in the early 1900s it was sufficiently adventuresome!

Lettuce Salad

1 head of lettuce, leaf or iceberg
3 chopped green onions
French Dressing
lemon juice
sugar

Put a layer of finely cut lettuce in a bowl, then a layer of chopped onions. Add 1 to 2 spoons of dressing, a good dash of lemon juice and a sprinkle of sugar. Fill up the bowl like this and let stand for a few minutes. Then take two forks and toss it all together. Use plenty of dressing and lemon juice and sprinkle over the top a finely minced hard boiled egg. *Serves six.*

French Dressing

½ c salad oil
2 tbsp vinegar
½ tsp paprika
1 tsp sugar
¼ tsp dry mustard
1 tsp salt

Place all ingredients in a bottle and shake vigorously. Chill. Shake again just before serving.

We thought the amount of spicing in this recipe a little heavy handed, so we reduced the amounts of paprika, mustard and salt. Ketchup (2 tbsp) may be added for a thicker dressing.

Pickled Beets were a common accompaniment to red meat dishes in the early 1900s. They suit both the Lamb Stew and the German Pot Roast in this chapter very well.

Pickled Beets

Scrub well 8 cups of young beets. Leave on tail and one inch of stem. Boil in salted water until very tender. Slip off skins under cool water. If beets are very small, leave them whole. Otherwise, slice them uniformly. Put in sterilized glass jars and pour the following hot mixture over them.

2 c	white vinegar
1 c	water
1 c	white sugar
1 tsp	*black peppercorns*

Boil the above for 5 minutes, then pour over beets in jars. Seal. Use after three weeks.

Nora (Campbell) Lefurgey was an old friend from Cavendish, P.E.I., who shared afternoons at the beach with Maud, picnicking, swimming and photographing. This light, simple dessert is reminiscent of their youthful, carefree rambles along the water's edge.

Nora's Pudding

2 ½ c	milk
¼ c	sugar
3 tbsp	cornstarch
¼ c	cold milk
15	marshmallows
pinch	salt
	pineapple, chopped
	coconut, *flaked*
	whipped cream

Scald milk in top of a double boiler. Stir into the scalded milk a quarter cup sugar.

Dissolve cornstarch in the cold milk and stir *into hot milk and sugar. Cook and stir in double boiler* until thickened. Remove from fire and stir in 15 marshmallows until dissolved. Add a pinch of salt.

Pour into mould *and chill.* Serve cold with some chopped pineapple underneath *each* helping, *flaked* coconut sprinkled over and *topped with a dab of* whipped cream.

Serves 4 or 5.

This is a classic in Maud's collection. Mock Cherry Pie was made frequently because it was Stuart's all-time favourite. While there isn't a cherry to be found, that is definitely the flavour you'll taste!

Mock Cherry Pie

1 c	raisins, chopped
1 c	cranberries, chopped
1 c	cold water
2/3 c	sugar
2 tbsp	flour
1 tsp	vanilla

Raisins and cranberries can be chopped together in a wooden bowl, but not too fine.

We suggest pulsing cranberries in a food processor, and leaving raisins whole.

In a saucepan, stir raisins, cranberries, water, sugar, and flour well together and boil 15 minutes. *Let cool slightly*. Flavour with vanilla.

Turn filling into an 8-inch pastry-lined pie plate. Moisten edge with water and cover with a top layer of pastry. Trim pastry. Crimp edges together around rim. With a sharp knife make a few attractive cuts in top pastry to allow steam to escape.

Bake at 425°F for 15 minutes. Reduce heat to 375°F for another 15 to 20 minutes or until crust is golden and filling bubbly. Serve with a dollop of whipped cream.

At Crawford's we use this rich filling in tarts, and we have reduced Maud's original one cup of sugar to two-thirds of a cup.

Down Home Favourites

"Home again! And the same old miracle has taken place. The moment I set foot on the red Island soil it *was* 'home' – I had never been away! And oh, how lovely and – lovelier – and loveliest – it is. How *satisfying!*"

Montgomery was rapturously in love with Prince Edward Island and its natural beauty. She grew fond of places in Ontario, too, but the Island was always home. It was the place of her birth, the place of her family, a place of "haunted loveliness" that she responded to with an intensity of appreciation unknown to most mortals. Very likely its magnificence grew the longer she remained in Ontario; visits home to favourite places and the companionship of family and friends restored some balance to her life. Maud returned to the Island, with Chester and Stuart in tow, as frequently as possible. Sometimes she spent a few days with Fanny (Wise) Mutch, a schoolgirl chum from Prince of Wales College who had a summer bungalow in Brighton. Aunt Christie, Ewan's sister, often had Maud come to stay for a day or two in Kinross. Maud spent a large portion of her holiday at Green

Macneill's Pond, mistakenly called the Lake of Shining Waters by many, as seen from the top of the sand dunes at the Cavendish shore.

Gables with Myrtle and Ernest Webb and their family, and at Gartmore Farm, the home of her cousin, Alec Macneill and his wife May. Both Cavendish homes were blessed with a good supply of cats and kittens, creatures Maud adored. At Alec and May's farm she encountered Good Luck, a kitten who would return to Ontario with her and the boys. "They have three beauties here of which one is the most oddly and beautifully marked cat I have ever seen – silvery gray with jet-black marks. The marks on his sides resemble a clover leaf with an M inside it and I said he would bring good luck so Chester suggested we call him that. I am going to try to take him home. I will not likely ever have such a chance again. Besides I want another cat from Gartmore Farm. The breed is good!"

L.M. Montgomery holding her favorite cat, Good Luck.

Maud had grown up very close to Green Gables with her grandparents Lucy and Alexander Macneill. Her home had fallen into disrepair with the death of her grandmother and Maud's marriage and relocation to Ontario; soon after, it was torn down. Consequently, Maud's notion of home was built heavily of familiar wood paths and lanes, beloved stands of spruce, hills and fields and birch groves. But home was also with her kin. Aunt Annie, one of her mother's sisters who Maud held quite dear, lived at Park Corner, where Maud had spent a good part of her youth in the company of her cousins, Clara, Stella, and Frede. She and Ewan were married in Aunt Annie and Uncle John Campbell's home by the Reverend John Stirling in 1911. Maud seemed to wind up many of her Island sojourns at Park Corner, a home known for boundless hospitality and excellent meals.

On one particular return home in October of 1932 Maud was staying at Green Gables when Myrtle gave an old Island goose supper, with stuffing and turnips. In spite of the inclement weather, it was quite a merry evening, with a food-laden table and the company of kin. That night "it rained hard and Myrtle and I sat in her cosy living room and read and talked and did fancy work, with a couple of cats to do our purring for us, while the rain splashed against the panes and the wind made wild music, and afar off the gulf boomed." It was a treasured evening home, with Myrtle's goose supper at the core.

In 1939 Maud's visit to Green Gables coincided with that of Marion, who was visiting with her daughter Elaine.

Along with special places and beloved people, food is an immediate and vital ingredient in Montgomery's fond memories of home. Satisfying meals are inextricably bound up with the pleasures of the island, and many recipes from the excellent cooks in her family made their way to Ontario with Maud. Cooking the food that she had enjoyed at so many tables was a way of keeping touch with the people of her earlier years, of revisiting happy occasions and acknowledging the family and home that she had been born into. Maud's later visits home grew bittersweet as people aged and passed away, and old haunts became overgrown. But the recipes she used from "home" provided a direct link with earlier times, rooting her in that special place even as time altered the landscape.

In the manse kitchen in Norval, Maud spent a March day making a fruit cake, and in memory kept company with her grandmother, who had shown her how to do it years before. "Somehow, making fruit cake always makes me think of Grandma. Once a year, in the fall, Grandmother made a big fruit cake, which always lasted the year out. It was quite an event. The evening before the fruit was prepared, Grandma washed the currants and I proudly stoned the raisins – for there were no 'seeded' raisins for the buying in those days. Next morning 'we' concocted the cake. Grandma brought out the spare-room washbasin, washed and scalded it very carefully and used it to mix the cake in with her bare hand – which is really the only way to mix a fruit cake properly. I helped beat eggs and hovered around watching everything with fascinated eye. When it was mixed completely the big cake pan with the peak up the middle was brought out, lined with greased brown paper and filled with the mixture. Invariably two little 'patty pans' were filled also – 'to see what the cake would be like' – but *they* were always given to me to eat as soon as they were cooked. Meanwhile I could scrape out and eat what was left in the mixing bowl. Despite its uncooked condition it was delicious – so thick was it with fruit and so rich with spices."

Grandmother Lucy Macneill's kitchen in the Cavendish homestead where Maud lived from the age of 21 months until her marriage in 1911 at the age of 36.

This chapter is full of Maud's down home favourites. The echo of long silent voices would have been more audible for her than for you and me, but try some of her recipes and listen closely!

Down Home Favourites

Menu

Baked Haddock

Baked Potatoes

Broccoli with Mock Hollandaise Sauce

Tomato Cocktail

Aunt Annie's Lemon Pie

Fannie's Doughnuts

Alternatives

Succotash

Codfish Cakes

Highland Scones

Scotch Shortbread

Christmas Cake

Park Corner Ribbon Cake

Fish was more often fried or poached than baked, so this is a fancier treatment than the usual.

Baked Haddock

3 lb	haddock
2 *c*	fine bread crumbs
1	tomato
2 tbsp	butter
	salt, pepper, sugar

Dress haddock. Remove head and tail and dredge fish with salt and pepper. Lay on fine crumbs in a greased shallow baking dish and sprinkle thickly with crumbs and dots of butter.

A peeled tomato is cut into 8 sections and is laid in a row lengthwise on fish. Each section is sprinkled with pepper, salt, sugar and a bit of butter.

The whole is set in a hot oven *(450°F)* until the fish is well cooked and nicely browned.

Allow 10 minutes baking time per inch of thickness of fish. Serves six.

Garnish with cress or parsley.

Baked Potatoes

6 *baking potatoes*

Choose long potatoes. Clean and rub with fat. Bake a full hour *at 380°F.* Do not put them too close together. Pinch the potatoes (using towel if too hot) to be sure they are soft and mealy all through. Make a crosswise cut through the skin on top of potato to allow steam to break through. Sprinkle salt on loose mealy white top and then stand a piece of butter on each top. It will quickly melt and be carried through. *Serves six.*

Tomato Cocktail

For convenience we are replacing the 1 quart of canned tomatoes in this recipe with 5 cups of tomato juice.

5 c	*canned tomato juice*
½	bay leaf
1 tsp	salt
¼ tsp	celery salt
1 tbsp	lemon juice

Mix all ingredients except lemon juice together. Bring to a boil and simmer for 10 minutes. Strain through a fine sieve and add 1 tbsp lemon juice. Cover and set in refrigerator to chill. *Serves six.*

Broccoli with Mock Hollandaise Sauce

For the broccoli:

Trim 1 ½ heads of broccoli, discarding woody parts of stems.

Steam until tender crisp. Serve drizzled with Mock Hollandaise Sauce. Serves six.

A traditional Hollandaise Sauce does not contain either flour or milk. Maud has added both, in the form of a white sauce, to her Mock Hollandaise Sauce to keep it stable while cooking or standing.

Mock Hollandaise Sauce

Make a medium white sauce using:

2 tbsp	*butter*
2 tbsp	*flour*
¼ tsp	*salt*
1 c	*milk*

Melt butter slowly. Add flour and salt and mix until smooth. Remove from heat and add milk. Return to heat and cook, stirring, until thick. Yields one cup.

1 c	medium white sauce
2	egg yolks
½ tbsp	lemon juice
2 tbsp	butter

Beat the egg yolks in the top part of a double boiler. Add the hot white sauce to the beaten egg yolks, cooking over hot water until smooth and thick. Add lemon juice and butter. This sauce does not curdle while standing as real Hollandaise is apt to do.

"WAS THERE ever such a house as Uncle John Campbell's for 'spreads'? Aunt Annie and her girls were all resplendent cooks and Uncle John C. had always the old Montgomery traditions of lavish hospitality."

Aunt Annie's Lemon Pie

2	egg yolks
1	lemon, grated rind and juice
1 c	sugar *(we advise using only 3/4 c)*
2 tbsp	flour
pinch	salt
	a small piece of butter *(2 tsp)*
1 c	sweet milk
2	egg whites, stiffly beaten
1	unbaked pastry crust *(see Chapter Three)*

Beat the yolks and add the grated rind and juice, the sugar and flour mixed together, the salt and butter. Stir in the milk. Fold in the stiffly beaten egg whites.

Pour into a raw pastry crust. *Start the pie in a 425°F oven for 5 minutes, then reduce heat and continue to* bake about 40 minutes in a moderate *(350°F)* oven. Watch it carefully as it browns quickly. It should be pale golden brown.

This really is a lemon sponge. It should be eaten while still warm because the filling will separate slightly on standing.

Fannie Mutch was an old school chum of Maud's; their friendship continued throughout their lives. She must have been very particular; in her recipe she has counted out the number of strokes the batter should receive after each addition. Thank heavens for electric mixers!

Fannie's Doughnuts

1 c	sugar *(halved)*
2 ½ tbsp	butter
3	eggs
3 ½ c	*all purpose* flour
4 tsp	baking powder
1 tsp	grated nutmeg
OR 2 tsp	grated lemon peel
1 ½ tsp	salt
1 c	milk
~1 c	flour

Cream butter and half the sugar together. (75 strokes)

Beat eggs till light and add the remaining sugar to them. (50 strokes)

Combine the two mixtures. Sift the flour with the baking powder, nutmeg and salt. Add it to the mixture alternately with milk by thirds, 50 stokes after each. Finish with 25 strokes.

Then add enough more flour to make a soft but not sticky dough – 1 c is generally enough.

Chill the dough for at least half an hour at this point making it easier to roll.

Roll out ⅓ of mixture first to ½-inch thickness. Cut out *with a floured doughnut cutter.*

Do not let doughnuts stand long after being rolled out.

Fry in 4 inches of oil in a deep fat fryer. Fry only a few at a time in order to keep the oil temperature between 360°F and 370°F. Turn only once. The doughnuts are done when they rise to the top and the underside is brown. Drain on paper towels. Sprinkle liberally with granulated sugar.

Add dough trimmings to half the remaining mixture and repeat.

Serve doughnuts warm. They reheat well in only a few minutes on a tray set in a moderate oven, 350°F. Yields about 2 dozen.

Succotash was a popular supper dish during the potato harvest, at the end of September, as it was fast and easy to prepare. Corn cut from the cob, half-dried beans (in the process of being dried for the winter), milk and butter were the main ingredients of the Webb recipe. Succotash was served as a meal of itself, and it does provide a balanced protein. You may wish to consider it a vegetable dish.

Succotash

3 c	beans *(we suggest dried lima beans, and only 2 c)*
1	can of corn *(cream style, 14 oz)*
1 c	good milk *(½ c only)*
1 tbsp	butter
	pepper and salt

Soak beans all day or night or at least 4 hours. *Cover beans with 2 inches of water.*

Bring slowly to the boil and let simmer *uncovered* until they break open. Keep enough water on them to cover and when nearly cooked let boil away. Add corn, milk, butter and pepper and salt to taste. *Serves six.*

We tried this recipe using only 2 cups of beans and only ½ cup of milk, which gave the consistency of thick chowder. Leftover cooked, diced sausage may be added.

Pickled beets always accompanied Codfish Cakes at Green Gables (see recipe Chapter Five), but recently one of the younger Webbs strongly expressed the view that Green Tomato Chow (Chapter Seven) was the condiment of choice for this dish. Such is the way families' traditions adapt and change! Salt cod was primarily a winter meal when fresh cod was not available. It must be soaked overnight in at least three changes of water to flush away the extremely high levels of salt. A chopper or food grinder is not necessary to shred the fish; a fork and your fingers will do quite nicely.

Codfish Cakes

2 c	salt codfish run through chopper
2 c	mashed potatoes, heaping
1	egg
½ tbsp	butter
	pepper to taste

Mix *all ingredients* well with butter and beaten egg. Shape this into round flat cakes and fry *in butter or bacon fat* till well browned. *Serves four.*

Maud has written "very good" *beside this recipe in her book. Half a cup of jam is enough to spread between the layers.*

Highland Scones

2 c	all purpose flour
4 tsp	baking powder
2 tbsp	sugar
1 tsp	salt
5 tbsp	crisco
2	eggs, well beaten
½ c	milk
	jam or marmalade (may use Plum Jam from Chapter One)

Sift dry ingredients. Blend in shortening *with a fork or fingers.* Stir in eggs and milk *with a fork.* Spoon dough onto oiled *(buttered)* paper dusted with flour. Pat with hands to ¼ inch thickness, *forming a large rectangle.* Spread jam or marmalade over half the dough, cover with the other half *by sliding your hand under the paper and lifting.* Press layers gently together. Cut into squares and then into triangles. Baste (brush) with milk to give a rich brown glaze.

Bake in a hot *(450°F)* oven for 10 to 12 minutes. Serve hot for tea or breakfast.

Serves ten or twelve, depending on the size of the triangles.

Alternatively, you may omit sugar and spread dough with ¾ cup grated cheese or pimento cheese and the scones are good to serve with a salad.

Although fruit sugar is called for in this recipe, Maud indicates that she prefers light brown sugar, so we have followed her preference. We baked a batch using bread flour and another using all purpose flour; there was no appreciable difference in texture.

Scotch Shortbread

1 c	butter
½ c	light brown sugar, packed closely in cup
2 c	flour
pinch	salt

Cream butter till very light. Gradually work in sugar. Work in flour and salt gradually.

Turn dough out on a lightly floured board and knead till it cracks. Press into ungreased tin 10 inches square. Prick surface all over with a fork and bake in a slow oven *(275°F)* about 25 minutes.

We recommend a 9x13 inch pan and an increased baking time of 40 to 45 minutes.

Maud has several recipes for Fruit Cake in her recipe book; this is the one we make at Crawford's, and it has been met with nods and murmurs of approval all around. The old hand-turned food grinder she refers to has practically been replaced today with the electric food processor, which certainly saves on elbow grease. But at Crawford's we bring out the old food grinder when its time to prepare the citron, the lemon peel, and the dried figs for this cake; it really does give a better texture to those ingredients than would a food processor. However, we have compromised on the raisins. Instead of the old style of seeded raisins we use seedless sultanas just as they are.

Christmas Cake

5 lb	*(12 ½ c)* seeded raisins run through chopper
1/2 lb	*(1½ c)* mixed citron and lemon peel ditto
1/2 lb	figs ditto
1 lb	*(2⅓ c)* brown sugar
1 lb	butter
12	eggs
1 c	syrup or fruit juice
½ tsp	*baking* soda
½ c	brandy or strawberry preserves
1 lb	*(3 ½ c)* flour
½ lb	*(1 ½ c)* almonds, blanched and chopped
1 tsp	each, of lemon, vanilla and almond flavourings

Mix fruit and peel and nuts with some of the flour. Cream butter and sugar well. Add eggs well beaten and beat until sugar is dissolved. Add syrup, soda and preserves *and flavourings.* Then add flour and fruit. Steam three hours and then bake 2 hours in a very slow oven. It can be baked in a slow oven all the time but steaming is best.

A shallow pan of hot water placed on the bottom of the oven will satisfy Maud's recommendation for steaming, and the baking time will be reduced by dividing the batter between smaller pans; use four 9x5 inch metal loaf pans or three 8-inch tube pans. Grease pans well and line them with a double layer of brown paper, cut to fit. Then grease the paper. Bake at 275°F for about 2½ to 3 hours.

Park Corner, the home of Maud's Aunt Annie and Uncle John Campbell, had a pantry that was never empty of good things to eat, like this cake!

Park Corner Ribbon Cake

½ c	butter
2 c	white sugar
4	egg yolks, slightly beaten
3 ½ c	pastry flour, sifted before measuring (add 2 tbsp for an electric oven)
5 tsp	baking powder
¼ tsp	salt
1 c	milk
4	egg whites, well beaten

Cream the butter and sugar and add the yolks of eggs slightly beaten. Sift together the flour, baking powder and salt. *Add the dry ingredients to the creamed mixture alternately with the milk, beginning and ending with dry ingredients.* Finally fold in the whites, well beaten. Divide the mixture into 3 equal parts.

Flavour one *part* with vanilla *extract, ½ tsp.* Flavour one part with lemon *extract, ½ tsp.* If liked, one of *these* white layers can be coloured pink.

To the third part add: ½ tsp cloves, ½ tsp allspice, 1 tbsp molasses, ⅔ c raisins, cut in pieces *(chopped raisins make for a cleaner cut).*

Bake in square cake tins *(3 greased and floured 8x8 inch tins at 350°F for 30 minutes).*

Put layers together with jelly or jam. *Or you may layer and ice the cake with orange icing (recipe follows). The spiced layer should be in the centre.*

Orange Icing

3 c	icing sugar
1	orange
1 tbsp	butter
1 tsp	lemon juice (optional)

Cream sugar and butter. Add grated rind and enough juice to make icing of the right consistency to spread. This is enough for both icing and filling. A teaspoon of lemon juice can be added.

Growing Up at Green Gables

In 1889, Green Gables was a working farm of 180 acres, long and narrow, with its north end touching the sea. Part of John Macneill's original 500 acre farm, it was owned by David and Margaret Macneill. The brother and sister kept livestock and raised crops in fields separated by woodlots, stands of bush that were so kept to provide firewood and lumber. Wood lanes, as they were called, led into the bush for access. As they were not heavily travelled they became some of Montgomery's favouite places to walk. A brook through the farm ran into a pond, called Macneill's Pond, which actually stretched to the dunes across a neighbouring Macneill farm. There, at the base of the sand dunes, a small trickle of fresh water from the pond wound its way to the gulf, its course altered each time the tide receded. Green Gables was fairly isolated, bordering on the spectacular North Shore, with its broad, hard sand beach and rocky cliffs.

Green Gables was never a happier place than the years that the Webb children were growing up.

In that year, Montgomery was living with her grandparents, Lucy and Alexander Macneill, on a neighbouring farm to the east, within easy walking distance of Green Gables. Her grandparents kept the post office in their kitchen, and the local one-room schoolhouse was just across the road. She had already spent many happy hours in "Pierce's woods." Pierce Macneill owned the farm just behind the school containing a wooded area that stretched over Green Gables farm as well, all the way to the brook. It was immortalized as the "Haunted Wood" in Maud's writings. Here as well, Lover's Lane wound off through the trees, connecting the farm to a field deeper into the woodlots.

Brother and sister Margaret and David Macneill with their grand-niece Myrtle, her husband Ernest Webb, and their daughter Marion, 1908.

Nine years her junior, Myrtle Macneill (Maud's third cousin) lived through her teen years at Green Gables with her great aunt and uncle, Margaret and David. Those years with considerably older, quiet, hard-working relatives must have been similar in tone to the years that Maud lived with her grandparents, giving them much in common. After Myrtle married Ernest Webb, they returned to live at Green Gables and their daughter, Marion, was born there in 1907. Myrtle cared for Margaret and David through their declining years, even as she had begun raising Marion, Keith, Anita, Lorraine, and Pauline.

Self-sufficiency was the order of the day in those years. The Webbs lived a fairly simple lifestyle, common to most rural folk, growing their own food, milking cows, raising pigs and chickens, and working the land with horses. Oil lamps and candles lit their evenings; wood burning room stoves were their source of heat through the long cold winter. Quilting, knitting, crocheting, rug-hooking and fancy work with embroidery were regular evening pastimes in this Baptist household. Fortunately the Cavendish District School was quite close; the children just had a short walk down across the brook and up through the Haunted Wood. The Webbs grew magnificent flower gardens, lavishing as much time and care on their dahlias, phlox, peonies and poppies as they did on their vegetable garden. Arrival of the long awaited Dominion Seed Catalogue in the mail each winter was cause for a flurry of optimistic planning for the upcoming season.

Ernest, Myrtle, Marion and Keith, in 1911.

There was a strong sense of community amongst the people living on farms and small enclaves around Cavendish. Neighbours kept an eye out for each other and were always ready to help when problems arose. Folks regularly dropped in unannounced and were always made welcome. Both a Baptist and a Presbyterian church flourished in Cavendish, and the church was the backdrop for many social events. Although Maud was a Presbyterian, she went to social gatherings at both churches. Once she was older, she gave elocutionary performances at the Baptist church and was noted for her skills in dramatic recitation.

Myrtle began her family several years before Chester was born, but the young cousins played well together whenever Maud brought her sons to the Island. One June afternoon Ernest rowed a group of them down the length of the Macneill pond, where they all climbed out to spend some time at the shore, wading in the tide. Of that day, Maud wrote: "After dinner while Stuart was asleep Ernest rowed Chester, Marion, Keith and me down the pond to the shore and we had a delightful afternoon. Chester had his first experience of paddling and, though he hung back very suspiciously at first, he enjoyed it after being thoroughly initiated. Not only did the minister's son go paddling but the minister's wife went too. In the snap Ernest took of us I fondly believed I had hidden my legs – but there is an odd number, as anyone can see!"

Keith Webb recalls one of Maud's visits just as strawberries were ripening in the garden between the old orchard and the lane. Young Chester, seven or eight at the time, was forbidden to set foot in the strawberry patch, probably due to Maud's concern over his potential for overindulgence. After an unexplained absence, Chester appeared with his pants pockets full of strawberries, red stains down the front of his pant legs, and strawberry juice trickling into his boots. He hadn't, he assured his mom, been in the strawberry patch. A different sort of paddling than what they'd all done at the sea suggested that Maud thought otherwise.

Ernest Webb took this picture of Maud, Chester, Marion and Keith during an afternoon by the sea. Maud genteelly attempted to hide her legs but acknowledged that an odd number were visible.

Childhood for Marion and her siblings was imbued with a deep appreciation for the natural world. They had a keen interest in growing things, and the challenge of finding the mossiest bank, catching the biggest fish, or discovering the best trove of spruce gum never ended. They were well versed with the rhythm of the seasons and felt spring's exhilarating freedom as they helped with planting, then tore off into the woods to spy on squirrels or hunt for mayflowers. School, work, and play all fell in step through the day without formal arrangement, and most of the chores could be made into considerable fun. There is sporting challenge to fishing, even if one has serious intentions of cooking the catch within the hour. The shore was a delight, scrabbling over rocks to find gulls' nests, wading barefoot in the shallows, jumping waves as they broke, or digging clams from their burrows in the sand. Cranberries grew wild at the base of the dune where the run from the pond flowed into the sea. They were there for the picking, which was fun for a while. The younger ones would drift off to play in the dunes, or in the warm, shallow, fresh water run where crabs and other interesting creatures made their home.

Marion and her brother and sisters were happiest outdoors, except for Anita who was hard to keep away from mixing bowls. Marion named a lane for herself, keeping it as a special place much the same as Maud had done with Lover's Lane. In Marion's Lane there grew a small clump of pink lady slippers, the delicate and elusive provincial flower, which she guarded carefully. Marion and Maud exchanged letters regularly, and Marion once mailed to Ontario a small box containing little branches of the ground spruce that grew in Lover's Lane woods, knowing that its fragrance would slip Maud back to her beloved lane for a few moments.

Lorraine and Marion with their early morning catch of brook trout.

As the five Webb children grew up there were more and more people curious to see Green Gables, the real life model for the Green Gables of Montgomery's imaginary tales. At first the travellers would come just to have a peek at the house and chat with the Webbs, but as the flow of visitors increased, the Webbs realized a demand for accommodation and began to take in boarders in the mid-1920s. The roof over the kitchen had been raised in 1921 to enlarge the second floor, providing more space for the family of five growing children. Ernest built two small cottages, and when the children's rooms were occupied with guests, the kids slept out in them. If demand was particularly great, guests took over the cottages too, and Marion, Keith, Anita, Lorraine and Pauline had to bed down in the machine shed!

A view across the brook to the Haunted Wood where Maud loved to roam.

Boarders would stay for a week, sometimes two, and tended to return year after year. Many would come a great distance to spend an idyllic holiday enjoying the spirit of the place that Maud loved. The sea was close by, the hospitality was warm, and the food was fresh and wholesome. The Webb girls had grown old enough to help with meals, and they divided up the chores amongst themselves. With her retiring nature, Marion tended to stay in the kitchen. By the time she was ten, Lorraine was setting the tables and serving guests. Anita "couldn't pass a sugar bowl without stirring it," and early on began asserting herself as the natural born cook that she was.

The shore was favoured as the summer meeting place of their Young People's Group. Meetings were held around a fire on the beach in the evening, with no lights nearby to interfere with the blaze of stars overhead. Maud attended one of these evenings, and told the story of the Marcopolo, a crippled ship whose captain ran it aground during a furious storm in order to save the crew and payload of planks. Maud was seven and in school when everyone heard the crash of a huge iron mast going over. The ship foundered along the North Shore for a day and a night, with anxious locals lining the water's edge. The crew was rescued the next morning, and while no lives were lost to the darkness and the waves, the drama of the disaster made rich storytelling for years after.

Marion left her childhood home in 1934 to marry Murray Laird and live in Ontario. In September of 1935 she and Maud heard, by letter, of the government's plans to establish a National Park at Cavendish, expropriating Green Gables and both adjacent Macneill farms to do so. Both Maud and Marion were heartbroken. In her journal, Maud wrote "I feel dreadfully. Where will the Webbs go? Another home I have loved blotted out…" Plans called for the establishment of a golf course at Green Gables and the other two farms, with Ernest as Park Warden. While it was agreed that Ernest and Myrtle would live out their days at Green Gables, operating a tea room in the house, it meant that their old way of life was over.

The Webb family, with Anita, Keith, Marion, Myrtle and Ernest in back, and Pauline and Lorraine in front.

In April of 1939 Maud wrote to Myrtle, requesting that Anita come to Toronto and be her companion-housekeeper and chauffeur. She would pay Anita $25.00 a month, with Sunday afternoons off, and assured Myrtle that she would treat Anita like a daughter. Maud made note that there was a good bus service to Norval, so Anita could easily visit Marion and Murray. Before the end of June, Anita travelled to Toronto by train and moved into Maud's home, by then on Riverside Drive.

Myrtle and Ernest were suddenly and unexpectedly asked to leave Green Gables in December of 1946, the day after Ernest turned 65. The whole community was shocked. The family's generations-long ties to the Green Gables farm were abruptly severed.

But life has a funny way of playing out as it should. Myrtle and Ernest bought the Baptist parsonage, in Cavendish, which had been built by the same man who had built Green Gables. The floor plan was identical, except that the staircase ascended the second floor from the opposite direction. Myrtle's granddaughter owns the house now, and her great-grandaughter celebrated her wedding with a reception in that new-old home. Splendid Island food was served – lobster, big plates of mussels, and more, all prepared by younger generations of the same family, still graced with the knack of making things taste good.

Pauline, Marion, Lorraine and Anita, early 1930s.

Growing Up at Green Gables

The recipes in this chapter are all Green Gables recipes from Marion's and Lorraine's collections, some of which appear in Aunt Maud's recipe book as well. Maud would have enjoyed them while visiting Green Gables; they are typical Prince Edward Island recipes, simple, wholesome and tasty.

Menu

Baked Beans with Boston Brown Bread

Myrtle's Pudding Cake

Sugar Cookies

Alternatives

Grilled Mackerel on the Beach

Salmon Loaf

Green Tomato Chow

Anita's Sweet Rolls

Plum Puff

Baked beans were a popular Saturday supper at Green Gables when the days were chilly and there was a gentle all-day fire in the kitchen stove. Grown, dried and stored in burlap bags, yellow eye beans were favoured for slow cooking to a mellowed richness in the oven, while the Boston Brown Bread steamed on top of the stove.

Baked Beans

2 c	yellow eye, navy, or soldier beans
1/3 lb	salt pork
1	medium onion, diced
1/4 c	brown sugar
1/2 c	molasses
1 tsp	dry mustard
1 tsp	salt
1/4 tsp	pepper

Wash beans and soak overnight in water to cover by two inches.

Next morning bring to the boil and simmer gently for about an hour, removing foam as it gathers on top. Drain, reserving liquid.

Slice the salt pork and put half the slices in the bottom of a crockery bean pot. Add half the beans. Add the rest of the salt pork, the onions and then the balance of the beans.

(A younger generation of the Webb family like to add a peeled, sliced apple with the onions.) Mix together the brown sugar, molasses, mustard, salt and pepper and about 1/2 c of reserved bean liquid, and pour over the beans. Add more liquid to cover the beans.

Bake covered in *a 250°F* oven for about 8 hours, adding more water as necessary to keep beans covered. For the last hour uncover the beans and stir gently once in a while to brown the beans. *Serves eight.*

Molasses is the common ingredient in the go-together recipes of Baked Beans and Boston Brown Bread. It came in gallon crocks and was poured over griddle cakes or just on bread as a snack. Molasses was used to sweeten many Island recipes as neither corn syrup nor maple syrup were readily available.

Boston Brown Bread

1 c	graham or whole wheat flour
1 c	yellow cornmeal
½ c	once-sifted flour
1 tsp	salt
¾ c	seedless raisins
1 tsp	baking soda
½ c	dark molasses
2 c	thick buttermilk

Combine the first five ingredients. Mix the soda and molasses together and add the buttermilk. Stir slowly into the dry ingredients, combining until smooth.

Spoon batter into greased baking powder tins until they are ¾ full. Tie on a double layer of waxed paper with a pleat in it for expansion. Place on a rack in a deep kettle and pour boiling water to fill ⅔ of the way up the tins. Cover kettle and steam rapidly for 2 hours. Add more boiling water as required.

Yields four 12 oz. cylindrical loaves.

Milk was provided courtesy of the Webbs' cows, and butter was too, after Ernest had finished with the heavy, arduous task of churning. They were fairly self-sufficient; once Myrtle wrote with some pride that they'd had to purchase only 10 pounds of butter in the whole year, which was some feat with a large family and the customary liberal use of butter in that era.

Maud herself had an amusing childhood memory of a particularly uncooperative batch of milk that tested her grandmother and Aunt Emily's patience for hours; they finally gave up, resigned to feeding the wretched batch to their pigs. Five-year-old Maud determinedly took a turn with her young arms and was elated to hear Aunt Emily exclaim in surprise that Maud had "brought the butter." And the pigs missed out!

Myrtle's Pudding Cake

2 tbsp	butter
1/2 c	white sugar
1/2 c	brown sugar
2	eggs
1 c	milk
1 tsp	*vanilla*
2 c	flour
4 tsp	*baking powder*
1/2 tsp	*salt*
1 quart	*crushed strawberries sweetened with 1/4 c sugar*

Cream butter and sugars. Add eggs and beat well. Sift flour, baking powder and salt together and add to mixture alternately with the milk and vanilla.

Put half the batter in a greased 8x8 inch pyrex pan. Spread with a layer of crushed strawberries and sugar. Not too many berries (1/3 c). Then a *remaining* layer of batter.

Bake 30 to 35 minutes at 350°F. After taking out of oven put a layer of crushed fruit on top and serve with cream. A box of berries or less is quite enough. *Serves eight.*

If, like Chester, you think that "enough berries" is never enough, you may want to increase this estimate. We do!

A well-known staple from old kitchens; light-textured with a subtle flavour.

Sugar Cookies

1 c	sugar
1/2 c	shortening (or half shortening, half butter)
2	eggs
7 tsp	cream or milk
2 1/8 c	flour
1 tsp	cream of tartar
1/2 tsp	*baking* soda
1/2 tsp	salt
1/2 tsp	nutmeg
1 tsp	vanilla
	coarse sugar for sprinkling, if desired
24	large raisins

Cream shortening and sugar together well. Add eggs and mix well. Sift dry ingredients together and add alternately with milk. Add vanilla and mix well. Chill dough.

Roll out on floured board to 1/4 inch thick. Cut with a cookie cutter and transfer to a greased cookie sheet with a spatula. Put a big raisin in the center of each cookie. *Sprinkle cookies with coarse sugar if desired.*

Bake at 375°F for 10 to12 minutes or until the edges are just starting to brown.

Makes two dozen 2 3/4-inch cookies.

Marion and Lorraine remember piling their two-wheeled, horse-drawn cart high with brush and driving it down to the beach to start a fire for cooking mackerel on a grill. Guests would then be taken down to the shore in the hay wagon for supper on the gulf's edge, with mackerel served spitting hot as the tide drew in or out and the seagulls wheeled overhead.

Grilled Mackerel

In place of the fire on the beach, your barbeque, preheated on high, will do. Put the fresh mackerel on the grill, reduce to medium-high heat and allow 10 minutes cooking time for each inch of thickness. Using a basket broiler makes turning the fish at half time easier. Fish is done when it turns opaque and starts to flake when a fork is inserted near the spine and twisted.

In August mackerel becomes fattier and will spatter and cause flare ups. That's when it's handy to have a barbeque with indirect heat; a drip pan with some water in it placed on the briquets solves the problem.

Now all you have to do is imagine the sand dunes on your left, the sea lapping on your right and the sand between your toes....

A dense loaf, which can be served warm or chilled.

Salmon Loaf

2	eggs, beaten
½ c	milk
1 c	bread crumbs
½ tsp	dry mustard
1 tsp	salt
1 lb	can of salmon
2 tbsp	vinegar or lemon juice
1 tbsp	parsley, chopped
2 tbsp	cracker crumbs
2 tsp	butter

Beat the eggs in a large bowl. Add the milk, bread crumbs, mustard and salt. Break up the salmon with a fork and add to the egg mixture. Stir in the vinegar or lemon juice, and the parsley and mix well with a fork.

Put all into a greased loaf pan. Sprinkle cracker crumbs over top. Dot with butter.

Bake at 350°F for 45 minutes. Serve warm with tomato sauce or cold with mayonnaise.

Serves six to eight.

Green Tomato Chow is frequently served with Codfish Cakes (see Chapter 6), which were made often at Green Gables. For Islanders, the two are a natural flavour combination, but you'll find that it is terrific with beef and pork as well.

Green Tomato Chow

9 lb	green tomatoes
6 lb	onions
8 c	brine (1 c pickling salt with 8 c water)
4 c	white vinegar
2 c	water
1	red pepper, chopped fine
5 ½ c	brown sugar
5 ½ c	white sugar
½ c	pickling spice tied loosely in triple layer of cheesecloth
2 tsp	prepared mustard
½ c	corn starch
1 tsp	turmeric

Put tomatoes and onions through coarse grind of a food chopper *or chop coarsely in a food processor.* Use enough brine to almost cover tomatoes and onions. Leave overnight. *The next day,* drain off brine. Add vinegar, water, red pepper, brown and white sugar and the bag of pickling spice. Simmer for 3 to 4 hours.

Mix mustard, cornstarch and turmeric together with enough vinegar to make a paste. Add to chow and cook another ½ hour, stirring frequently.

Have sterilized jars and caps ready. Pour into jars and tighten caps immediately.

Yields 10 16-oz jars.

Anita Webb made a career of cooking, and these rolls were served often.

Anita's Sweet Rolls

1	package dry yeast
1 tsp	white sugar
½ c	lukewarm water
½ c	milk
¼ c	shortening
¾ tsp	salt
¼ c	white sugar
2	eggs
2¾ c	flour

Soften yeast with 1 tsp sugar in the ½ c lukewarm water.

Heat milk to scalding. Combine with shortening, salt and sugar in mixing bowl. Stir and let cool to lukewarm. Beat the eggs well and add to the bowl with the yeast. Add the flour cup by cup, beating well with a wooden spoon after each addition. Dough should be soft but not stick to pan.

Turn out onto floured board and knead until smooth and elastic, about 10 minutes. Grease a large bowl, put dough in and turn it over so the surface is greased. Cover dough loosely with greased waxed paper and a clean tea towel. Let rise in a warm place until double in size, about 1 hour.

Punch dough down and divide into 2 round balls. Let rest on board, covered, for 10 minutes. Divide each ball into 10 pieces. Shape into little balls. Place 2 inches apart on greased cookie sheet. Brush tops with melted butter. Cover with greased waxed paper and a clean tea towel. Let rise in a warm place until double in size, about 45 minutes.

Bake at 375°F for 15 to 20 minutes. Makes 20 rolls.

To make cloverleaf rolls divide dough into smaller balls. Grease muffin pans and put 3 balls in each muffin cup.

If this recipe had been in Maud's recipe book she would have called it Mock Plum Puff because there are no plums in it! The version here is an offspring of the original Green Gables recipe, having passed through another Island kitchen.

Plum Puff

1 c	white sugar
½ c	shortening
1	egg
2 ½ c	flour
2 tsp	baking powder
½ tsp	salt
1 tsp	vanilla
½ c	milk

Cream sugar and shortening together well. Beat in egg. Sift and add dry ingredients alternately with milk and vanilla. Divide the dough in half and press half into a greased 9x13 inch pan.

Filling

3 c	raisins
	boiling water
¾ c	white sugar
2 tbsp	corn starch
1 tbsp	butter
½ tsp	vanilla

Put raisins in a saucepan and cover with boiling water. Bring to a boil. Mix sugar and corn starch together and add to raisins. Cook and stir until thickened. Add butter and vanilla. Let cool slightly and spread on bottom layer of dough.

Knead and roll the remaining dough on a well-floured board into a 9x13 rectangle.

The dough will be soft. Roll up on a rolling pin and unroll to fit over the raisin filling.

Sprinkle with coarse sugar. Bake at 350°F for 45 minutes. Serves twelve.

Festive Fare

Scrumptious goose dinners with all the trimmings were traditional celebratory fare on the Island, whether the occasion was Thanksgiving, Christmas or simply a long-awaited gathering of kin. Islander Michael Shaw, of the venerable *Shaw's Hotel* on Brackley Beach, P.E.I., says that his family always served goose at Christmas, always with cranberry sauce and always accompanied with turnips, mashed potatoes with gravy, and carrots and parsnips together. Aside from being experienced and hospitable hoteliers and excellent cooks, the men in the Shaw family are excellent marksmen, so the geese that have graced their table over the years were generally wild. Vegetables were always served mashed, and dessert was the ubiquitous Plum Pudding. That delectable menu seems to have been common to many Island households in the festive season, and is still served today without noticeable refinement. Maud's recipe book gives a wonderful account of how to prepare a goose, which we include in this chapter just in case you're ever presented with the opportunity to try it yourself.

Maud quite fancied duck at special meals too. "The seventh of November was Thanksgiving. Mrs. Mason was away so I cooked our duck dinner. My hand has not lost its cunning for Stuart said blissfully 'Mother, *no one* can make gravy like you' and 'Mother, why don't you always do the cooking?' Well, I wish I could for I love cooking when I have time for it. Mrs. Mason is a good cook but she hasn't 'the knack' in some things. All the Montgomerys had it and our family of Macneills through the Woolners. Grandmother Macneill knew naught of calories and vitamins or balanced rations but she was the best cook I ever knew in my life.

Aunt Annie was also a wonder and all her girls inherited the gift. We can all 'make things taste good' as Stuart says. We know by grace and not by law just how big a pinch to put in."

The year was 1927, long before Canadians began observing Thanksgiving on the second Monday of each October. For Chester and Stuart, Thanksgiving was welcome respite from their studies at Upper Canada College, and Maud's duck dinner made coming home all the more enjoyable.

For the Macdonald family the focus of Christmas was the Sunday School concert, which Maud helped to organize and present each year, usually on or just prior to December 24. Children and young adults of the church performed skits, gave readings and entertained the rest of the congregation, after practising for several weeks and holding a dress rehearsal. The church was always decorated with a Christmas tree, hung with presents for the young participants. Maud was quite involved with practises, and on performance night she often had to "arrange dialogues and 'run' tableaux and evolve order out of the chaos behind the scenes." A concert in 1919 at the church in Zephyr was particularly enjoyable: "To-day was very mild and when Ewan and Chester and I left after supper we positively enjoyed our drive over. Owing to the skim of snow the night was not dark. The road was good, the trees and fields and groves pleasantly suggestive and eerie and elusive, as if full of elfish secrets. Chester chattered amusingly and I enjoyed the drive. The concert and Christmas tree was also nice. Chester recited, Ewan read and acted as Chairman. I gave two

Maud standing in front of the dining room bay window of the Norval Manse, between the spirea bushes that she planted, 1930s.

readings and also read the Cottar's Saturday Night while it was shown in a series of tableaux – so I think the Macdonald family did its duty and quite deserved the nice fat goose which was hung on the tree for it. The first and only goose we have ever been given, as it happens!"

Christmas dinner was normally served on Christmas Eve, and was sometimes followed with the Sunday School concert. Maud "dressed up" a tree after the boys had gone to bed, and Christmas morning brought the happy discovery of gifts and a beautifully decorated tree, which certainly hadn't been there the night before!

A welcoming view of the Norval Presbyterian Church Manse's verandah.

Our festive fare menu includes raisin wine, which Maud made occasionally. She wasn't aware, when she laid one batch down to ferment, of the breadth of its appeal. "Made a grotesque little discovery today. Last January I made some raisin wine, put it in bottles and set them away in a dark corner of the jam closet to ripen. They had never been disturbed since but to-day while sorting out the shelves I noticed something odd about one of the bottles. I picked it up – looked at it – nearly 'swooned' in the good old fashion, in horror. The cork had blown out of it and, floating in the wine was a mouse – a very dead mouse – a large mouse – so large that I can't imagine how it ever got down through the very slender neck of the bottle. Perhaps it swelled after its demise! I hurled bottle, mouse and all down into the ravine. The other bottles were still corked and virgin. But I doubt if I shall ever be able to enjoy a glass of that wine, even when it is ready to be enjoyed. Ugh!"

But if you can manage to keep the mice from indulging, we still think that Raisin Wine suits a festive meal quite well!

Festive Fare

Menu

Roast Goose with Gravy and Stuffing

Cranberry Sauce

Mashed Turnips

Brussels Sprouts

Mashed Potatoes

Carrots and Parsnips

Thanksgiving Salad

Raisin Wine

Queen of Plum Puddings with Brown Sugar Sauce

Maple Creams

Parisian Sweets

Alternatives

Carrot Pudding with Brown Sugar Sauce

Mincemeat Necessaries

We've given Maud's directions for preparing and roasting a goose just as they appear in her recipe book. Don't be afraid to try it – she gives very explicit instruction, with a bit of an anatomy lesson, for the novice!

Roast Goose

Singe off all hairs and down by holding goose over burning twisted paper. Draw out any pin feathers. Cut legs off at joints. Make incision through skin below breast bone just large enough to admit hand. Remove entrails and cut out vent. Be careful not to break gall bladder which is attached to the liver. The lungs and kidneys are attached to backbone and care must be taken that every particle of them is removed. Introduce fingers under skin close to neck and remove wind-pipe. Draw down neck skin and cut off neck close to body, leaving skin long enough to fasten under back. Remove oil bag in tail and wash bird by allowing water to run through it.

Scrub outside of goose with brush and cold water but do not allow it to soak in cold water. Wipe it dry inside and outside. If there is any disagreeable odour wash inside and outside with soda water. Fill body and breast with stuffing. Roast, allowing 20 minutes to the pound – goose weighed after dressing and before stuffing. Before putting goose in oven rub with butter, pepper and salt.

When goose is done make gravy as follows. Pour off all the fat into a bowl. Then put back in pan 8 tbsp fat and stir into it with a whip 8 tbsp flour. Cook and stir until fat has completely disappeared leaving only a brown flour mass. Have ready hot water and stir 8 cups into gravy. Season with salt and pepper.

Goose is a very fatty fowl with dark meat. Prick the skin well and set it on a rack in an open roasting pan. It does not need basting and fat should be removed from the pan as it gathers. Roast to 190° F on a meat thermometer.

An 8–10 lb goose will serve 8 to 10 people and will require 3 to 4 hours of cooking time at 325°F.

A variation in the customary all-bread stuffing, Maud's version adds mashed potatoes to the bread crumbs. Double quantities for a goose.

Stuffing for Duck or Goose

This amount is sufficient for one duck. When doubled use only 1 egg.

2 c	hot mashed potatoes
1 1/4 c	stale bread crumbs
1/4 c	finely chopped salt pork
1	finely chopped onion
1/3 c	butter
1	egg
	pepper, salt and savoury to taste

In Cavendish cranberries grew wild at the foot of the dunes. Picked in the fall, they would keep in sacks in a cool room for several months.

Cranberry Sauce

2 c	sugar
2 c	water
4 c	cranberries

Put sugar and water on together and boil for 5 minutes. Add the cranberries, cover and let stand off fire for 5 minutes. Then boil 5 minutes. Keep tightly covered till cool.

Maud's recipe book contains very few vegetable recipes, probably because vegetables were so simply prepared. Our Island friends at Shaw's Hotel have contributed the traditional vegetable recipes they have served with roast goose for generations.

Mashed Turnips

Slice a yellow turnip, cut off skin and dice. Cover with boiling salted water and cook until tender, about 20 to 25 minutes. Drain and mash with 1 tbsp butter, pepper and salt to taste. A 2 ½ lb turnip will serve six.

Brussels Sprouts

Select uniform sized brussels sprouts. Trim off stems and outer leaves. Rinse well.

Pour boiling water over, just enough to cover, and cook until tender but not soft.

Stir in 1 tbsp butter and a squeeze of lemon juice. 2 lb will serve six.

Mashed Potatoes

Peel 6 medium potatoes and cook in boiling salted water until tender. Drain well and mash. Warm 1 tbsp butter and 2 tbsp milk together and beat into potatoes until fluffy. Add salt and pepper to taste. New potatoes are not suitable for making fluffy mashed potatoes. Serves six.

Carrots and Parsnips

Wash and scrape equal amounts of carrots and parsnips. Cut in uniformly sized pieces. Cook together in boiling salted water just to cover, until tender. Drain and mash together with 1 tbsp of butter, and salt, pepper, and nutmeg to taste. If you'd like a change from the Island habit of mashing all vegetables, just toss the pieces in butter and seasonings. 1 ½ lb of each vegetable will serve six.

Tart and refreshing, with a nice crunch!

Thanksgiving Salad

2 c cranberries
1 c sugar
1 c water
1 c walnut meats
3 stalks celery
1 apple
juice of half a lemon
juice of half an orange

Stew and sweeten the cranberries. *Bring 1 cup of water and 1 cup of sugar to the boil. Add the 2 cups cranberries and simmer until they pop, about 10 minutes. Chill.*

Cut nuts and celery in small pieces and dice apple. Mix all thoroughly and add lemon and orange juice. Serve on lettuce leaves. *Serves eight.*

And here it is! Maud's Raisin Wine – loved by all!

Raisin Wine

1 lb	raisins *3 c*
1 gallon	cold water *20 c*
2 lb	white sugar *4 1/2 c*
1 tbsp	*dry* yeast or 1 yeast cake

In a stainless steel or enamelware kettle, simmer raisins in the water for 1 hour.

Strain through a colander, and return liquid to kettle. Dissolve sugar in liquid *and let cool to lukewarm.* Rub raisins through a sieve and add raisin pulp and yeast *to liquid in kettle.*

Let vessel stand covered for 3 days. Strain *through triple cheesecloth* into jars.

Cover with cloth until fermentation ceases, then cork. Let stand 12 months before filtering into bottles.

Befitting its name, this rich, regal dessert is also abundantly portioned! Make it when you know you're having a crowd, and rest assured that leftovers will keep well.

Queen of Plum Puddings

½ lb	butter *(1 c)*
½ lb	sugar *(1 c + 2 tbsp)*
6	eggs
1 c	milk
1 ¼ lb	flour *(4 ¼ c)*
½ c	cider or fruit juice
1 tsp	nutmeg
1 tsp	cloves
1 tsp	mace
1 lb	seeded raisins, chopped *(2 ½ c)*
1 lb	dates, *chopped (2 ¾ c)*
¼ lb	shredded citron *(¾ c)*
½ lb	suet finely chopped (*1 ½ c*)

Beat egg whites and set aside. Cream butter and add sugar. *Cream well.*

Add well beaten yolks of eggs, then the milk. *Measure the flour and reserve ½ c.*

Next add flour alternately with the beaten whites. Add the cider and spices. *Mix in.*

Lastly add the suet and the fruit dredged lightly with *reserved* flour.

Place in a well greased pudding mould, cover well and steam for 6 hours. Serve with sauce. Delicious.

This requires a large pudding mould of 2 ½ quart capacity with a tight fitting lid. If your mould has no lid, cover with aluminum foil and tie tightly with string. Place on a rack in a steamer or deep kettle. Pour in boiling water until it comes ⅔ of the way up the sides of the mould. Cover the steamer, bring to the boil and maintain a reasonable boil for 6 hours, adding more boiling water as required to maintain level. Remove from steamer, let stand on a rack for 10 minutes. Unmould and cool completely before wrapping and chilling.

To reheat place the pudding back in its greased mould and cover again. Steam for 2 hours. Easily serves twelve.

Maud recommends this sauce to accompany the Queen of Plum Puddings, but if you're planning to serve ten or twelve we think you'll need to double this batch size so that all at the table can have as much sauce as they'd like.

Brown Sugar Sauce

½ c	brown sugar
2 tbsp	cornstarch
pinch	salt
2 c	boiling water
1 ½ tbsp	butter
1 tsp	vanilla

Combine sugar, cornstarch, and salt. Add boiling water gradually while stirring and cook for 10 minutes stirring constantly to avoid lumping. *Remove from heat.* Add the butter and vanilla. Stir until butter is melted and serve hot. *Serves six.*

Maple Creams

Take half as much water as maple syrup. Cook without stirring and when almost done put in a small piece of butter. When it soft balls* take from fire and stir rapidly until it becomes waxy. Roll into balls and enclose each ball between halves of walnut.

* *The soft ball test is done by putting a few drops of the hot mixture into a cup of very cold water and forming it into a ball with a fingertip. A candy thermometer indicates this stage at 235°F.*

Parisian Sweets

The food processor replaces the grinder nicely for this confection. 8 oz of each of these fruits equals 1½ c by volume for each. Maud's recipe calls for 1 lb of each, but that makes an extraordinary number of sweets, so we have halved her quantities.

8 oz *pitted dates*
8 oz *figs*
8 oz *raisins*
8 oz *walnuts*
powdered icing *sugar,* sifted

Grind fruit and nuts and mix thoroughly. Knead on board till moist. Work in as much powdered sugar as possible. Roll out, cut in squares or fancy shapes. Let ripen a few days *in a covered tin, layered between waxed paper.*

Open the door to the aroma of an old fashioned Carrot Pudding slowly reheating and you'll know its either Christmas or New Year's Day!

Carrot Pudding

1 c	grated raw potato
1 c	grated raw carrot
1 c	suet finely chopped
1 c	raisins
1 c	currants
1 tsp	*baking* soda
1 tbsp	hot water
1 ½ c	flour
1 tsp	cloves
1 tsp	cinnamon
1 tsp	salt
1 c	white sugar

(Potato, carrot, suet and raisins can be run through chopper instead of grating.)

Add the remaining ingredients in order given, dissolving the soda in the hot water before adding and sifting cloves and cinnamon with flour. Fill well greased pudding moulds ⅔ full and steam for 3 hours.

If you wish to make individual puddings, ordinary custard cups will do nicely. The cover of steamer should be curved rather than flat as a flat cover tends to drop moisture on pudding and make it heavy. Don't lift the cover if you can avoid it. If you have to add water use boiling water. If you have to cut a hot pudding use a string instead of a knife. Pudding can be made weeks ahead. In that case take it from mould, cool on wire cake cooler, wrap in dry towel and store in a cool dry place. When it is to be served return to mould and reheat thoroughly in steamer. Serve with brown sugar sauce. *See recipe this chapter.* Good. *Serves ten to twelve.*

Scribbled on the back of a meeting notice of the Canadian Women's Press Club is a list of "Mincemeat Necessaries," in Maud's handwriting. We found this curious paper tucked into her recipe book, although she had copied in to the book as well. The notice was for a luncheon in Eaton's Round Room, on College St. in Toronto, at 12:30 pm sharp on Wednesday October 13, 1937. The speaker was Margaret Widdemar, "one of the most successful novelists and fiction writers of the day. A popular poetess too. She will talk about her writing craft, give advice on marketing, etc., etc. Miss Widdemar's work appears in all the big magazines on the continent and this is a rare opportunity to hear one of the big fiction 'stars.' The fee was 50 cents, presumably including lunch.

We can only speculate that Maud attended, and further imagine an acquaintance whispering her notion of "Mincemeat Necessaries" to Maud during a lull in the proceedings. The real author of this recipe will never be known, but Maud enjoyed the result enough to include it in her collection.

Mincemeat Necessaries

1 1/2 lb	seeded raisins *(3 3/4 c)*
1 1/2 lb	suet *(4 1/2 c)*
1 1/2 lb	apples *(2 c)*
1/2 lb	citron peel *(1 1/2 c)*
3/4 lb	blanched almonds *(2 2/3 c)*
2 1/2 lb	currants *(7 1/2 c)*
2 1/2 lb	brown sugar *(5 2/3 c)*
1/2 oz	cinnamon ground *(1 tbsp)*
1/2 oz	cloves ground *(1 tbsp)*
1 c	fruit juice
1	nutmeg grated *(1 tbsp)*
1/2 oz	salt *(2 tsp)*
1/2 oz	allspice *(1 tbsp)*
3	lemons, juice and grated rind only

Run first 6 ingredients through *food* chopper and mix well with the rest in a stone crock.

Or chop first 6 items to a medium fine grind in a food processor, and mix with the rest. Traditionally mincemeat was stored in a covered crock placed on a cold basement floor, ready at any time to be made into pies or tarts over the winter months. Nowadays not everyone has a cold basement floor, so keep mincemeat refrigerated. Flavour improves and mellows with age.

Looking Back

Often our lives' greatest loves remain stories untold. Respect and quiet admiration are not sensational; grace and sensitivity and acceptance may be marks of great character, but despite their inspiration, they are often consciously acknowledged only in retrospect.

Maud's Aunt Annie was one such love. The only one of her mother's siblings to grant consideration and dignity to the motherless and eerily perceptive young Maud, Annie Macneill Campbell held an inviolable place in Maud's heart. She was endlessly welcoming, endlessly loving, and the strongest provider of a sense of family that Maud had. Her children were more sisters than cousins to Maud. She was not a worldly or well-known woman; when Maud brought her to Toronto she displayed a charming and unashamed naivete for the sophisticated activity of a big city. Maud felt that Aunt Annie's generous hospitality kept her run ragged, and sometimes wished that her aunt could slow down with her invitations, but this same generosity had produced wonderful meals that remained long in Maud's memory. Her death was one of Maud's deepest losses. Her story was poignantly preserved, after her funeral, when Maud sat alone in her old kitchen and carefully copied recipes from her cook book.

Annie Campbell, Maud's beloved maternal aunt who lived at Park Corner.

They were recipes she knew well, recipes that spoke volumes of a life happily spent, recipes that had united a broad range of Annie Campbell's family and friends. Of Aunt Annie's old cook book, Maud wrote: "It spoke very eloquently of her. Never was such a cook as Aunt Annie. Almost every page recalled some feast of the past."

Norval Presbyterian Church spire seen across the mill pond on the Credit River.

We all have memories of helping our mothers make special things to eat. This shared experience is more than basic training for life ahead; it grants an intimacy that establishes membership in a small and select group, usually the family. Appreciation of food is a common thread running through the most divergent families, but in these days of dual careers and easy availability of prepared foods, that bond becomes imperiled. Will tomorrow's children lead lives enriched with memories of growing and preparing food with their parents? Maud voiced the same concern as she recalled watching her grandparents making cheese in their old home:

"It is curious how old memories bob up. A phrase in what I have just written – 'the odors of supper seeping in from the kitchen' – makes me remember our old 'cook house at home.' This was a little building at right angles to the kitchen, with a plank platform between. It had been, I recall being told, the porch of the 'old' church in Cavendish – that is of the church that preceded the 'old' church I went to as a girl. . . .

"Every spring the cookstove – first the old 'Waterloo' and then the coal stove – was moved out to the 'cookhouse' and all the cooking done there for the summer. It must have meant a great many extra steps for the cooks but it kept the main house cool and free from flies – which was a desired thing in the days before screens. Many a good bite was cooked in that old spot. The shelves all around the walls were used as a pantry. Grandma kept her dried hams in a big box of oats in the corner and bunches of garden herbs and 'shalottes' hanging from the beams. Grandma made her cheese curds there, too, and put them into the 'hoops' which were then carried out to the cheese press at the corner of the orchard fence where a big gray stone served as a weight. Grandma was a 'master hand' at making cheese. It is a lost art as far as individuals are concerned. All cheeses nowadays are made in factories. And as a result they have not the flavor of the cheeses Grandma made. Something is lost when things are made *en masse.* I wonder if there is a single woman in Canada today who can make a cheese – unless it be someone in the 'foreign' colonies.

Lucy Woolner Macneill, Maud's maternal grandmother, with whom Maud lived until 1911.

"The mention of cheeses wakens another memory. It is evening. Grandmother and Grandfather are adjusting the cheese hoop under the press. I am standing by watching them and drinking in the loveliness around me. June was walking over the fields. The sun had just set and I saw that loveliest of all created things – a young moon in an amber evening sky."

Maud's grandparents were no longer living when memory carried her back to their side in the old apple orchard. And the Park Corner recipes that she copied kept Aunt Annie real and touchable too, just as Maud's own recipe book captures a fragment of her life for us. We can keep, and make again, the recipes that gave Maud pleasure, recipes that allowed her to enrich and satisfy other peoples' lives. Is there any greater legacy?

water and tomatoes + bring to boil.
Stir in 1 tsp soda + strain. Add 1 qt-
boiling milk, salt + pepper + 2 level
tb butter. Bring to a boil and serve.
Serves 12 people.

Hamburg Steaks

Run 1 lb. lean beef through chopper twice.
Season with salt, pepper + finely chopped
onion + ½ tsp nutmeg. Mix in one slightly
beaten egg. Shape into flat cakes and
fry in deep fat.

Canned Chicken

Kill, clean + put in tub of water over
night with a little salt to draw out
blood. Drain well, cut up + skin. Joint
legs at main joint and again at
middle. Cut all meat off breast. Pack in
jars. Put carcasses on in steamer,
cover with water + boil till scraps of
meat are cooked. Have jars sterilized.
Put on top of each a small tsp salt and
a little minced onion. Fill the bottles with
strained liquor from bones, put on rubbers
and lids, leaving a turn or two loose. Put
in boiler and boil for 3 hours. As soon as
cool enough screw tops tight. (Skim fat off
water as clean as you can and season
with salt + pepper.

Chicken Mould

Clean scraps off carcases + run them through
chopper. For every 7 cups ground meat use 3½ tb

Equivalency Tables

The following charts show approximate kitchen equivalents for converting standard measures into metric measures.

Volume Measures

Imperial	*Metric*	*Imperial*	*Metric*	*Imperial*	*Metric*
1/8 tsp	0.5 ml	1/4 cup	60 ml	4 cups	1 L
1/4 tsp	1 ml	1/3 cup	75 ml	5 cups	1.2 L
1/2 tsp	2 ml	1/2 cup	125 ml	6 cups	1.5 L
1 tsp	5 ml	2/3 cup	150 ml	7 cups	1.6 L
1 tbsp	15 ml	3/4 cup	175 ml	8 cups	2 L
		1 cup	250 ml		

Weight Measures

Imperial	*Metric*	*Imperial*	*Metric*	*Imperial*	*Metric*
ounces	grams	ounces	grams	pounds	kilograms
1 oz	28 g	8 oz	227 g	2 lb	0.9 kg
2 oz	57 g	12 oz	340 g	3 lb	1.4 kg
4 oz	113 g	16 oz	454 g	4 lb	1.8 kg
				5 lb	2.25 kg

Temperature Measures

Fahrenheit	*Celsius*	*Fahrenheit*	*Celsius*	*Fahrenheit*	*Celsius*
250° F	120° C	350° F	180° C	425° F	210° C
300° F	150° C	375° F	190° C	450° F	230° C
325° F	160° C	400° F	200° C		

Bakeware Measurements

	Imperial	*Metric*
	inches	centimeters
round cake pan	8 x 1 1/2	20 x 4
	9 x 1 3/8	20 x 3.5
tube pan	8 x 4	20 x 10
	9 x 4	23 x 11
pie plates	8 x 1 1/2	20 x 4
	9 x 1 1/2	23 x 4
square pans	8 x 2	20 x 5
	9 x 1 3/4	23 x 4.3
rectangular pans	9 x 5 x 2 1/2	23 x 13 x 6
	13 x 9 x 1 3/4	22 x 4 x 3

Sources for Quotes

Selected Journals are *The Selected Journals of L.M. Montgomery Volumes 1, 2 and 3* edited by Mary Rubio and Elizabeth Waterston, published by Oxford University Press in 1985, 1987 and 1992. The ten volumes of handwritten journals from which the "selected" journals are drawn are part of the "L.M. Montgomery Collection" in the University of Guelph Archives. All selections are published with the permission of the University of Guelph Archives and Mary Rubio.

FRONTISPIECE
"If I had not been... an excellent cook." Unpublished journals, Vol. 8, p. 95

INTRODUCTION
"I have never... of the case." *Selected Journals*, Vol. 2, p.364

CHAPTER ONE
"I have always enjoyed... pleasant time." unpublished journals, Vol. 9, p.96
"All day I worked... candles." *Selected Journals*, Vol. 2, p.366

CHAPTER TWO
"It was the smartest... with accoutrements." *Selected Journals*, Vol. 2, p.29
"I have been busy... quite sufficient bite." *Selected Journals*, Vol. 3, p.105
"I am keeping one eye... did the trick." *Selected Journals*, Vol. 3, p.18

CHAPTER THREE
"Early rising per... next day's canning." *Selected Journals*, Vol. 2, p.396
"Rise at 7:30... big fruit cake." *Selected Journals*, Vol. 2, p.397
"There was a general... country village." *Selected Journals*, Vol. 3, p.280
"Norval manse is well... behind the village." *Selected Journals*, Vol. 3, p.284
"I do like the electric... there is light." *Selected Journals*, Vol. 3, p.286
"We had an electric... eighty miles away." *Selected Journals*, Vol. 3, p.366
"I have begun preparing... a success." unpublished journals, Vol. 8, Nov 27 1930

CHAPTER FOUR
"I rose at six... something every minute." *Selected Journals*, Vol. 3, p.297
"ate the most delicious... in the gates." *Selected Journals*, Vol. 3, p.298
"Because we want... in our programs." *Selected Journals*, Vol. 3, p.300
"full of the Macdonald... she gave me." *Selected Journals*, Vol. 2, p.308

CHAPTER FIVE
"our wild exultant... fun of doing them." *Selected Journals*, Vol. 3, p.378
"Nora and I drove... really laugh." unpublished journals Vol. 8, July 2, 1932
"What do I like?... dandelion wine." *Selected Journals*, Vol. 2, p.370
"who would have delighted Dickens" *Selected Journals*, Vol. 2, p.81
"innocent sweetness" *Selected Journals*, Vol. 2, p.81

CHAPTER SIX
"Home again! And the.... How satisfying!" *Selected Journals*, Vol. 3, p.339
"haunted loveliness" *Selected Journals*, Vol. 3, p.135
"They have three beauties... is good!" *Selected Journals*, Vol. 3, p.139
"it rained hard... afar off the gulf boomed" unpublished journals Vol. 8, p.148
"Somehow, making fruit... with spices." *Selected Journals*, Vol. 3, p.394
"Was there ever such... lavish hospitality." *Selected Journals*, Vol. 2, p.123

CHAPTER SEVEN
"After dinner while... as anyone can see." *Selected Journals*, Vol. 2, p.253
"I feel dreadfully... blotted out." unpublished journals, Vol. 9, p.171

CHAPTER EIGHT
"The seventh of... pinch to put in." *Selected Journals*, Vol. 3, p.359
"arrange dialogues... behind the scenes." *Selected Journals*, Vol. 2, p.35
"Today was very mild... as it happens." *Selected Journals*, Vol. 2, p.359
"Made a grotesque... to be enjoyed. Ugh!." unpublished journals, Vol. 9, p.164

LOOKING BACK
"It spoke very eloquently... feast of the past." *Selected Journals*, Vol. 3, p.193
"It is curious how old... evening sky." unpublished journals, Vol. 8, p.95, 96

References

Harold McGee "On Food and Cooking"
First Collier Books Edition 1988
MacMillan Publishing Co., New York

"Five Roses. A Guide To Good Cooking"
Lake of the Woods Mills Ltd. 25th Edition

"Cavendish, Its History, Its People."
by Harold H. Simpson
produced by Harold H. Simpson and Associates Ltd., Nova Scotia

Acknowledgements

Our appreciation and thanks go to:
Marion (Webb) Laird, who had the foresight to collect a lifetime's worth of photographs and letters, and to carefully store Aunt Maud's handwritten recipe book, so that one day this book would be possible;
Professor Mary Rubio, University of Guelph, for her assistance, enthusiastic encouragement and sensitively drawn preface;
Edward and Margaret Boyce, Maya Mavjee, Chris Boyce, and Norman Holt of Moulin Publishing Ltd., who have shown unblinking acceptance of the project from the outset;
the Macdonald family, who have supported our familial interest in Maud and our shared appreciation for the foods she liked;
the Webb family, including Uncle Keith Webb, Aunt Lorraine (Webb) Wright, Aunt Anita Webb, Aunt Pauline (Webb) Jones, and cousins Louise Lowther and Ina Reed, who have related delightful anecdotes and dug through photo albums to help with this book;
Islanders Michael Shaw and Audrey MacKay, who have helpfully contributed their families' traditional recipes;
and many Norval folk, including Hardy Barnhill, Ethel Curry, Edna Davis, Lloyd Hustler and Mary Maxwell, who still remember the years Maud resided in our village.

Index

flat-cakes and fry till well browned

Never-Fail Pancakes.

8

2 cups bread flour, 4 [16] level tsps baking powder, ½ tsp salt, 2 [8] tbs sugar, 1⅓ or ¾ cups milk, 1 [4] egg, 2 [8] tbs soft or melted butter. Mix + sift dry ingredients. Beat egg, add milk + stir slowly into first mixture. Stir in butter. ~~Eff~~ If not thin enough add more milk. Drop by dessert-spoonfuls on hot un-greased aluminium fryer. When puffy full of bubbles turn. Don't mix cakes until ready to fry them.

Pork Chops + Spare Ribs

Put chops into baking pan with a thin slice of onion on each. Pinch of salt + dash of pepper. Pour a little water in pan + bake.

Scalloped Fish

Into a baking dish put a layer of cold mashed potatoes and on this a layer of cooked fish. Cover with a thin layer of cracker crumbs and repeat until dish is full. Have top layer of crumbs thickly dotted with butter. Pour over it enough milk to moisten and bake until silver knife comes out clean

Tomato Soup.

Take 1 qt. can tomatoes or 1 qt. raw skinned tomatoes. 1 qt. boiling water. If tomatoes are raw stew till soft. If not just mix